The Bloody Sunday Inquiry

The Families Speak Out

Edited and introduced by Eamonn McCann

Pluto Press
London • Dublin • Ann Arbor, MI

First published 2006 by Pluto Press
345 Archway Road, London N6 5AA
and 839 Greene Street, Ann Arbor, MI 48106

Distributed in the Republic of Ireland and Northern Ireland by
Columba Mercier Distribution, 55A Spruce Avenue,
Stillorgan Industrial Park, Blackrock, Co. Dublin, Ireland.
Tel: + 353 1 294 2556. Fax: + 353 1 294 2564

www.plutobooks.com

British Library Cataloguing in Publication Data
A catalogue record for this book is available from the British Library

ISBN   0 7453 2511 4 hardback
ISBN   0 7453 2510 6 paperback

Library of Congress Cataloging in Publication Data applied for

10 9 8 7 6 5 4 3 2 1

Designed and produced for Pluto Press by
Curran Publishing Services, Norwich
Printed and bound in the European Union by
Antony Rowe Ltd, Chippenham and Eastbourne, England

CONTENTS

Acknowledgements

This book was commissioned the Bloody Sunday Trust.

Among those whose support was important are Gemma Cairns, Tracey Collins, Patricia Coyle, Nuala Crilly, Tony Doherty, Seamus Farrell, Pat Friel, Ciaran Gallagher, Angela Hegarty, Jean Hegarty, Paul Hippsley, Kitty Holland, Luke Holland, Goretti Horgan, Matty Horgan, Catherine Kelly, John Kelly, Adrian Kerr, Paul McCauley, Conal FcFeely, Britt Madsen, Christy Moore, Hilary Morton, Jim O'Neill and Anita Villa.

The photographs of the interviewees are by Mark Willets. Other photographs courtesy of Hugh Gallagher, the *Derry Journal* and the Bloody Sunday Trust.

Eamonn McCann
September 2005

Chronology

The Bloody Sunday Inquiry was announced by British Prime Minister Tony Blair in a statement to the House of Commons on 29 January 1998.

The members of the Tribunal appointed to conduct the Inquiry were Lord Saville of Newdigate, Judge William Hoyt, former chief justice of the Canadian province of New Brunswick, and retired New Zealand judge, Sir Edward Somers. Somers withdrew for health reasons in July 2000 and was replaced by former Australian High Court judge, John Toohey.

Saville made his introductory statement at Derry Guildhall on 3 April 1999. Oral hearings began at the Guildhall on 27 March 2000, with the opening speech by Christopher Clarke QC, counsel to the Inquiry. The first witness took the stand on 28 November 2000.

The Tribunal ruled in December 1998 that military witnesses should be publicly identified, other than in exceptional cases. This ruling was reversed by the Court of Appeal in London in July 1999.

In August 2001, the Tribunal ruled that, other than in exceptional cases, soldiers should testify at Derry Guildhall. This ruling was reversed by the Court of Appeal in London in December 2001.

In May 1999, the Tribunal upheld an application from a number of police officers to give their evidence from behind screens. In February 2002, most of the other police officers scheduled to testify applied for and were granted screening. An application by lawyers for the families for judicial review of this ruling was rejected by the Northern Ireland Court of Appeal in March 2002.

The Inquiry moved to the Methodist Central Hall, Westminster, on 24 September 2002 to hear the testimony of British soldiers and others. Hearings continued at Central Hall until 21 October 2003. The Tribunal then returned to Derry, where hearings resumed on 29 October 2003. The main body of evidence was completed on 13 February 2004. In June 2004 two additional witnesses were heard. Clarke's closing speech was delivered at the Guildhall on 22 and 23 November 2004. The Tribunal sat briefly on 27

January 2005 to hear evidence from a final witness. In all, the Inquiry sat for 434 days.

The cost of the Inquiry was around £155 million.

The Tribunal's report is expected to be published in early 2006.

Lord Gifford (on the left) and Sir Louis Blom-Cooper   Lord Saville

TRIBUNAL MEMBERS

The Honourable Lord Saville of Newdigate (Chairman)
The Honourable Mr William Hoyt
The Honourable Mr John L. Toohey
(Mr Toohey replaced Sir Edward Somers, who retired on health grounds in July 2000.)

COUNSEL TO THE INQUIRY

Christopher Clarke QC
Alan Roxburgh
Cathryn McGahey
Bilal Rawat

Arthur Harvey QC, Barry MacDonald QC, Seamus Treacy QC, Michael Lavery QC, Karen Quinliven, Tom McCreanor, Ciaran Harvey, Brian McCartney and Fiona Doherty (instructed by Madden & Finucane) represented Gerard McKinney, William McKinney, Gerald Donaghey, Michael McDaid, John Young, Michael Kelly, Jackie Duddy, Kevin McElhinney, Hugh Pius Gilmour and John Johnston (killed); Joseph Friel, Joseph Mahon, Patrick O'Donnell, Patrick McDaid, Alana Burke and Damien Donaghey (wounded); and Patrick Campbell, Margaret Deery and Daniel McGowan (wounded, now deceased).

Lord Gifford QC and Richard Harvey (instructed by McCartney & Casey) represented James Wray (deceased).

Michael Mansfield QC and Kieran Mallon (instructed by MacDermott & McGurk) represented William Nash (deceased), Alexander Nash (wounded/now deceased) and Daniel Gillespie (wounded).

Michael Mansfield QC and John Coyle (instructed by Desmond J. Doherty & Co) represented Bernard McGuigan (deceased).

Declan Morgan QC and Brian Kennedy (instructed by Brendan Kearney, Kelly & Co) represented Michael Bridge and Michael Bradley (wounded).

Eilis McDermott QC and Mary McHugh (instructed by Barr & Co) represented Patrick Doherty (deceased).

Sir Louis Blom-Cooper QC and Paddy O'Hanlon (instructed by Francis Keenan) represented the Northern Ireland Civil Rights Association (NICRA).

Edwin Glasgow QC, Edward Lawson QC, Gerard Elias QC, Sir Allan Green QC and Rosamund Horwood-Smart QC (instructed by the Treasury Solicitors) were the lead barristers representing military witnesses.

Introduction

The smoke hadn't cleared from the Bogside when Captain Mike Jackson, second-in-command of the First Battalion of the Parachute Regiment, standing in the lee of the Rossville Street Flats, began pondering the notes that the Bloody Sunday families believe were to become the basis for a cover-up of murder.

Huddled in the houses and flats into which they had fled, looking fearfully out on the scene, neighbours of the dead were already resolving that, however long it might take, there'd be a reckoning.

In the Methodist Central Hall in Westminster more than 31 years later, in October 2003, General Sir Michael Jackson, as he now was, Chief of the General Staff, Britain's number one soldier, was explaining to Michael Mansfield, barrister for the families of some of the victims, that he could remember next to nothing about compiling the Bloody Sunday 'shot list' and could not explain why none of the shots described in his list appeared to conform to any of the shots actually fired.

This book is the Bloody Sunday families' account of how they succeeded in forcing Jackson and his soldiers and superiors to explain, if they could, in public and under oath, how and why they had killed or wounded 28 unarmed civil rights marchers in Derry on 30 January 1972.

The first official show of trying to establish the truth was phoney. On the day after the killings, Prime Minister Edward Heath asked the Lord Chief Justice, Lord Widgery, to conduct a public inquiry under the Tribunals of Inquiry (Evidence) Act, 1921. Widgery didn't waste time. He defined his remit narrowly, to cover events on 'the streets of Londonderry where the disturbances and the ultimate shooting took place' over 'the period beginning with the moment when the march ... first became involved in violence and ending with the conclusion of the affair and the deaths'. There was to be no examination of prior military or political planning or of suggestions of subsequent cover-up. Widgery sat on 17 days between 21 February and 14 March, hearing 114 witnesses, of whom 30 were Derry civilians. Hundreds of eyewitness statements, mostly collected by the Northern Ireland Civil Rights Association (NICRA), organisers of the 30 January march, were made available to Widgery and were ignored by him. Six of the 14 wounded were not approached for an account of how they'd come to be shot.

Widgery's selection of soldiers to give evidence was significant, too. Company Sergeant Major (CSM) Lewis, who had commanded Support Company of the First Paras, which probably fired all the fatal shots, made himself available to testify, but inexplicably, as it seemed at the time, wasn't called.

Widgery passed his 39-page report to Home Secretary Reginald Maudling on 10 April. It was published on 18 April, eleven weeks after the event.

Heath's government didn't wait for Widgery's hearings, much less his report, before disseminating its own version of events. On 1 February, as Widgery's appointment was being announced in the House of Commons, British Information Services (BIS) was distributing to wire services and broadcasting outlets across the world a document headed 'Northern Ireland: Londonderry' telling that, 'Of the 13 men killed, four were on the security force's wanted list …. One man had four nail bombs in his pocket …. Throughout the fighting that ensued, the army fired only at identified targets – at attacking gunmen and bombers …. The troops came under indiscriminate firing.'

The document ended with a list detailing 14 separate shooting incidents which it suggested made up the 'fighting'. These were the 14 incidents on the 'shot list' in Jackson's handwriting, which was to come to light more than three decades later.

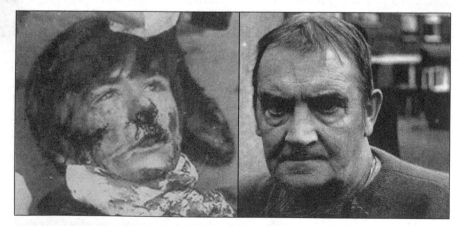

Michael Quinn (left) and Daniel Gillespie (right), both wounded

Widgery's report endorsed the Jackson/BIS account, in effect exonerating the paras. It concluded that the soldiers had been fired on as they moved into the Bogside to carry out an arrest operation against rioters, that their return shooting – if perhaps, in some instances, striking the wrong targets – had been in accordance with their standing orders, and that these standing orders were satisfactory.

'Soldiers who identified armed gunmen fired upon them in accordance with the standing orders in the Yellow Card [issued to all soldiers in the North at the time, setting out the circumstances in which they were allowed to open fire]. Each soldier was his own judge of whether he had identified a gunman .... At one end of the scale, some soldiers showed a high degree of responsibility; at the other, notably in Glenfada Park, firing bordered on the reckless. These distinctions reflect differences in the character and temperament of the soldiers concerned.'

As many as six of the dead may have been 'firing weapons or handling bombs', Widgery suggested. His key conclusion, the basis of newspaper headlines and political commentary proclaiming 'Paras cleared!' was that: 'There is no reason to suppose that the soldiers would have opened fire if they had not been fired on first.'

The Royal Ulster Constabulary (RUC) was meanwhile conducting a parallel investigation. The perfunctory nature of this exercise is indicated by the fact that, again, a number of the wounded were not interviewed. On 4 July 1972, the police file was passed to the North's Director of Public Prosecutions. In a written answer to a parliamentary question on 1 August, the British Attorney General declared that, together with the Northern Ireland DPP, he had concluded that the evidence didn't warrant prosecution of any soldier.

In the same month, in Dublin, Jack Lynch's Fianna Fail government – badly damaged by mass street demonstrations in the immediate aftermath of the killings – attempted to append the Bloody Sunday issue to an already-lodged application against Britain claiming breaches in the North of the European Convention on Human Rights. The European Commission rejected the application on procedural grounds.

In August the following year, an inquest in Derry into the deaths returned an open verdict, the only finding possible within NI law at the time. Addressing the jury after accepting the verdict, coroner and local solicitor Hubert O'Neill commented:

> It strikes me that the army ran amok that day without thinking what they were doing. They were shooting innocent people. The people may have been taking part in a march that was banned, but

that does not justify the troops coming in and firing live rounds indiscriminately. I would say without hesitation that it was sheer unadulterated murder. It was murder.

O'Neill's trenchant characterisation of the killings was welcomed by the bereaved families and more widely. But it had no standing in law. The official version remained that the soldiers had been justified in opening fire and killing or wounding the victims.

Following the inquest, the families issued civil actions for compensation in the Northern Ireland High Court. The actions were settled in 1974 on the basis of a government statement which, citing Widgery, repeated that: 'The troops acted lawfully and in self-defence and in order to protect their comrades when they opened fire on the gunmen and bombers who had attacked them.' The statement went on to acknowledge that none of the dead had been proven to have been among the gunmen and bombers and that all were therefore entitled to be regarded as having been found not guilty of such charges. Documents published by Saville were to reveal that the Ministry of Defence (MoD) and the Home Office had agreed to this acknowledgement following advice from officials that they would be unable to sustain the allegations against the victims if the issue came to trial. Unaware of this background – the official advice was withheld from the families – solicitors advised that the government statement was as favourable an outcome as could be achieved and that ex-gratia payments ranging from £250 to £16,500 should be accepted. Announcing that the civil claims were being withdrawn, the solicitors declared that the families now wanted a new inquiry into the deaths. There was no legal or political follow-up and no formal government response. It was to be a decade and a half before the Bloody Sunday families were again to operate or be represented as a group.

The campaign which emerged in the early 1990s and which was to lead to the establishment of Saville intrigued some and angered others. Why Bloody Sunday? There have been bigger death tolls in single incidents in the Troubles. Fifteen Catholics died in the Loyalist bombing of McGurk's Bar in the New Lodge area of Belfast in the month before Bloody Sunday. Eighteen paras died in an IRA ambush at Warrenpoint, Co. Down, in 1979. And, numbers apart, was not the IRA killing of eleven Protestants as they stood in reverent silence around the Enniskillen war memorial on Remembrance Sunday in November 1989, for example, as wicked and cruel as the Bogside massacre?

A number of things made Derry different. Part of the motivation for the massacre may have been to shore up Unionist rule: Northern Ireland

Prime Minister Brian Faulkner was under mounting pressure from supporters of Dr Ian Paisley and from within his own Ulster Unionist Party to secure a much tougher law-and-order strategy from the British, swiftly to put an end to illegal marches against internment and to smash the Bogside no-go area, from which state forces had been excluded since the internment raids of the previous August. But all key decisions relating to Bloody Sunday were taken by British political and military chiefs. Unionist input was minimal. Blame for the Bloody Sunday killings could not be ascribed to the communal hostilities of Northern Ireland. This was a very British atrocity, and the biggest single killing by state forces in the course of the Troubles. The resultant affront was compounded by the fact that the British state at the highest level, in the person of the Lord Chief Justice, had then proclaimed that the killings were neither wrong nor illegal. In every other atrocity with which Bloody Sunday has regularly been compared or likened, the victims are acknowledged, more or less universally, as having been wrongly done to death and the perpetrators damned as wrongdoers. But the Bloody Sunday families were told, in effect, that while they might personally, reasonably, lament the loss of a loved one, they had no wider ground for grievance or legitimate expectation of the killers being punished. The state stood by its own. All the dead were thus diminished. Liam Wray, brother of Jim, 22, shot in the back at point-blank range as he lay wounded in Glenfada Park, commented: 'It said that my brother was less than fully human.'

The fact that this second injustice had been inflicted by the official custodian of constitutional truth drove the insult deep.

Bloody Sunday, moreover, to an extent that isn't true of any other atrocity, proved a pivotal plotpoint in the narrative of the North's Troubles. Generally, communal heartache in the wake of mass killings has tended to dissipate over time, the lives of individuals left behind likely shattered forever, but public life not discernibly changed. In contrast, a consensus

Joseph Friel, wounded

among commentators and historians holds not only that the paras' action in Derry had an immediate political motivation – to shore up the Faulkner government by reasserting the rule of British law – but also that the plan spectacularly backfired: far from bringing the Bogside back within the Queen's Writ, the killings catapulted the area, and other Catholic–Nationalist districts across the North, outside all notions of constitutionality. The Northern Parliament, which had operated at Stormont since partition in 1921, was abolished by order of the Westminster government eight weeks after Bloody Sunday, three weeks before publication of Widgery's Report. No other major change in the last 35 years can be seen as having stemmed so directly from a single incident. This fact, that Bloody Sunday had a clear and lasting political significance to match its magnitude as a human event, helped give the families' campaign for the truth an added capacity many years later to reverberate in the wider political world.

Bloody Sunday differed from other atrocities, too, in that it was perpetrated in full public view. Most killings in the North, as always in conflicts of the kind, happen with thunderclap suddenness, on lonely roads or in the dead of night, typically by stealthy ambush or furtive bomb. Bloody Sunday unfolded over a period of perhaps ten minutes in a built-up area in broad daylight and in circumstances in which thousands of the victims' friends and neighbours were crowded into the immediate vicinity. Every killing and wounding was witnessed, some at very close quarters. Within hours, even as Jackson was transmitting his fraudulent account to Whitehall, which was to be disseminated by BIS to deceive the world, people in Derry were piecing their memories of the day together and assembling their unshakable truth.

Estimates of the numbers on the Bloody Sunday march varied wildly at the time, from the BIS's 3,000 to NICRA's 25,000. Perhaps 12–15,000 would be near enough. Of these, four-fifths, at a minimum, will have been from Derry. A sizeable percentage of the town's population, then, including a high proportion of the 30,000 residents of the immediate Bogside–Brandywell– Creggan area, had been involved personally in the event which was to climax in the killings. There were few local people who didn't know some member of the families of the dead. Bloody Sunday had the character not merely of a politically inspired state atrocity but of one that inflicted shared, communal injury and a mass sense of bereavement. The community thus marked could not consign the experience unassuaged to the past. (This aspect of Bloody Sunday was crucial in ensuring that Saville would have to hear hundreds rather than scores of Derry witnesses, and therefore a commensurate muster from the military, extending the length of the Inquiry and setting the taxi meters of the legal teams awhirring for years: it was the brazenness of the atrocity, more than any other single factor, which dictated the cost of the Inquiry.)

The communal aspect of the injury didn't prompt the Bogside to turn its face entirely away from the world and nurse its grievance to itself. Minutes after the shooting, Bernadette McAliskey (then Devlin) declared that 'This is our Sharpeville.' The identification with the South African township where 69 demonstrators had been gunned down by police in 1960 was more than a facile flourish. In a speech a few months earlier in Derry, she had made lengthy comparison between Long Kesh in Antrim – which held the internees whose release was to be the sole demand of the 30 January march – and Hola Camp in Kenya, where thousands of Kikuyu had been brutalised during the 1952–60 'Emergency'. Oppression in Northern Ireland was of an altogether lower order of intensity than in colonial Kenya or apartheid South Africa. But in the terror and rage of Rossville Street on the day, the parallels were pertinent. The tendency of those who came through Bloody Sunday to see the experience reflected in conflicts elsewhere, past and present, was to be a continuing feature of remembrance of the massacre in years ahead.

Conservative voices in Britain and Ireland regularly argued during the course of Saville's Inquiry that the elaborate enterprise was likely to prove futile because 'people have already made their minds up'. They had a point, although not the point they thought they had. Campaigners in Derry hadn't demanded a new inquiry because they wanted to be told the truth, but because they wanted the truth to be told. They didn't need a report from Lord Saville to find out what happened, but to find out whether the state would acknowledge what happened. The fact that lies have been substituted for a known truth doesn't make the search for acknowledgement of this truth futile, but on the contrary lends it an insistent urgency.

In the first two years after the killings, NICRA organised commemoration marches on the Sunday closest to 30 January. In 1974, the chairperson of the local NICRA branch, life-long housing and human rights campaigner Brigid Bond, unveiled a monument to the victims in Joseph Place in the shadow of the Rossville Flats, which remains the centrepoint of Bloody Sunday commemorations. But partly as a result of Bloody Sunday, the axis of agitation in the early 1970s was shifting from civil rights to communal conflict and anti-state action, and NICRA's presence was fading. From 1975 until 1989, the Bloody Sunday march was organised by Sinn Fein. Family members marched in the front rank every year. But not all families took part. Some disapproved of the political colouration.

In the years between 1974, when the civil claims were settled, and the beginning of the 1990s, the demand for a new inquiry wasn't a prominent or regular item in the North's political agenda. The call would be reiterated in ritual fashion at the end of each annual march, then largely forgotten for another twelve months. Militant Nationalist politics in the period, on the face of it, sought an end of British jurisdiction in Northern Ireland, not justice from within the British legal system. There was no campaigning organisation representing the families and seeking vindication of the Bloody Sunday victims as a cause in itself.

In 1987 a small group of relatives, initially prompted by Tony Doherty, son of Paddy Doherty, 31, who had died in Joseph Place after being shot from behind as he crawled away from the shooting, came together to discuss a new push for a second inquiry. At the outset, the group comprised six to ten people meeting monthly in a tiny office at a Sinn Fein centre in Cable Street in the Bogside. Eventually named the Bloody Sunday Initiative (BSI), the group took over organisation of the annual march in 1989. One reason was that Doherty and others (despite Doherty himself being a Republican ex-prisoner and a member of Sinn Fein) realised that if the campaign was to succeed it would have to be made accessible to individuals and interest groups outside Republicanism. Another had to do with the introduction of the Public Order Act, requiring organisers of marches to seek permission from the police, else all who

Peggy Deery, wounded

participated would be liable to prosecution: previously, only march organisers were at risk. This proved an effective piece of legislation and – which may have been part of the intention – put Sinn Fein in an awkward dilemma. Asking the RUC for permission to march still ran directly against the Republican grain. But so did asking thousands of supporters to put themselves at hazard to make a point through a party event. It was easier all round that a campaigning group without ideological baggage should collect police permission and continue the march. The move might be seen, too, as symbolic of a shift back from outright rejection of the legal and constitutional system, and tentatively towards the pursuit of remedies within the system.

However, if family members were beginning to take the lead in the campaign, not all families, and few of the wounded, were actively involved. The right of the BSI to speak for 'the families' was to be occasionally, sometimes heatedly, contested. Probably inevitably, this was to be a recurring feature of the campaign. Meantime, broad political developments and the approach of the 20th anniversary fuelled determination and helped spread support. Alert to new opportunities, the BSI was anxious to break out from the rigid confines of ritualised protest.

The run-up to the 1992 anniversary was marked by publication by Brandon Books of *Bloody Sunday in Derry – What Really Happened*, commissioned by the BSI and edited by the present writer, profiling each of the dead and denouncing Widgery as a liar and an accessory after the fact of murder, and calling for a new inquiry. The BSI was also closely involved in making a 30-minute Channel 4 television documentary, directed by local film-maker Margo Harkin and presented by Bogside women's activist Maureen Shiels, arguing that until Widgery was repudiated it would remain unreasonable to expect the Bogside and areas like it to endorse the rule of law. Two mainstream documentaries challenging the Widgery account were transmitted on Channel 4 and BBC1. Newspaper features pegged on the 20th anniversary proliferated. There was a palpable sense in Derry of the issue moving back centre stage. The turnout on the 1992 march was the largest since Bloody Sunday itself.

Aiming to seize the mood of the moment, the BSI called a meeting the following week in the Pilot's Row community centre in Rossville Street, with a view to broadening further the base of support and recruiting new activists. The attendance – perhaps 50 – was somewhat disappointing. The new mood hadn't solidified yet into a movement. But still, 33 people, double the number and from somewhat more diverse backgrounds than the existing group, signed up on the night. Fifteen members of eight of the families were joined by half a dozen Sinn Fein activists, two members of the local trades council, a member of the Socialist Workers' Party, artist Colin Darke, Johnny Walker of the Birmingham Six, radical Quaker Robin Percival, and others. Four of the 33 were English. This was the Bloody Sunday Justice Campaign (BSJC), which was to carry the campaign forward for the remainder of the decade.

As the BSJC fixed its sights on winning a second inquiry, the broader human rights issues with which the BSI had begun to grapple were assigned to a new group, the Pat Finucane Centre (PFC), named after the Belfast solicitor who in 1989 had become one of the victims of a Loyalist paramilitary gang under the secret joint command of the British Army intelligence group, the Force Research Unit, and the security service, MI5. (In February 2005, as an adjunct of 'police reform', New Labour was to give MI5, notwithstanding its involvement in terrorist murder, overall control of intelligence operations in the North.) In effect, the BSI had evolved into two separate, complementary organisations.

The demands of the BSJC agreed at the Pilot's Row meeting were for the repudiation of Widgery and the institution of a new inquiry; a formal acknowledgement of the innocence of the victims; and the prosecution of those responsible for the deaths and injuries. Later disagreements were foreshadowed when Catholic bishop Edward Daly explained that he couldn't endorse the third demand. Dr Daly was one of the iconic figures of Bloody Sunday for his grace under fire as he led a group carrying the body of Jackie Duddy, 17, shot from behind as he fled the inrushing soldiers in the Rossville Flats car park, out of the Bogside. He wrote to BSJC chairman John Kelly, brother of Michael Kelly, 17, shot dead as he stumbled from a rubble barricade on Rossville Street:

Over the years, I have made several appeals on behalf of local men who were involved in the conflict in the 1970s. They left this jurisdiction because police were seeking to arrest them …. They desperately want to return home …. While the cases are not exactly the same, I believe that if I were to take a different position in the case of those who murdered members of your families, it would appear to be inconsistent and might weaken the case I have made on (the local men's) behalf.

The issue was later to re-emerge in fears that pressing for prosecutions might undermine the demand for 'amnesty' for Republican 'on the runs' as part of the peace process.

Weekly meetings of the BSJC were not all smoothness and light. The most regular references in the minutes are to pleas from members that others respect the chair. Personality differences and arguments over strategy apart, the fraught nature of the proceedings had something to do with an increasingly crowded agenda. 'The more we got done, the more there was to disagree about,' recalls one wry veteran of the period. Family members in particular began to acquire recognition, even some standing in Derry, a development that had an occasional downside. Michael McKinney, brother of William, 27, shot dead as he stood with his hands above his head in Glenfada Park, is one of those who recalls being 'chased' from doors as he tried to collect a petition in Creggan by residents who assumed that anyone campaigning on Bloody Sunday must somehow be associated with the IRA. John Kelly was bemused to be approached by people seeking help with housing problems.

Perhaps sensing a stirring, local MP John Hume wrote to Prime Minister John Major in mid-1992 supporting the relatives' case. Major replied, referring to the statement issued when the civil claims had been withdrawn 18 years earlier: 'The Government made clear in 1974 that those who were killed on "Bloody Sunday" should be regarded as innocent of any allegation that they were shot whilst handling firearms of explosives.' There was some indication that Major had high hope that this might dispose of the matter. But to

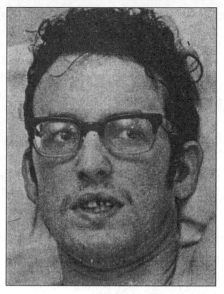

Michael Bradley, wounded

the relatives, Major's statement had merely sharpened the question: the fact that the victims were now acknowledged by the British prime minister as innocent surely underlined the need for explanation of why they had been shot. Northern Ireland Secretary Patrick Mayhew further stiffened resolve by subsequently rejecting an interviewer's suggestion that Major, having conceded the victims' innocence, ought now to offer an apology: 'An apology is for criminal wrong-doing and there is nothing in the Widgery Report to support that, and therefore it would be wrong.'

Not everyone in Ireland confidently approached by the families responded in a positive way. Of more than 30 TDs invited to a Dublin hotel across the street from the Leinster House parliament for the launch of the Bloody Sunday Trust's (BST's) 20th anniversary book *Bloody Sunday In Derry* ... only one, Tony Gregory (Independent), showed up. The Irish President, Mary Robinson, famed feminist campaigner and future UN Human Rights Commissioner, twice refused to meet the BSJC. Eventually she did receive a delegation, after John McKinney and Tony Doherty had paraded for a number of hours in protest outside her residence, Árás an Uachtaráin. The Catholic cardinal, Dr Cathal Daly, likewise declined to meet the group. And Derry City Council, then dominated by the Social Democratic and Labour Party (SDLP), deployed legal technicalities to justify a refusal to support the campaign financially.

On the other hand, encouragement came from unexpected sources. In the BBC documentary, *Remember Bloody Sunday*, CSM Lewis of Support Company, whose offer of evidence had been declined by Widgery, volunteered that he hadn't seen any civilians with guns or bombs on the day, that he believed all the deceased had been unarmed, and that he knew of at least one soldier who had fired more rounds than he had officially been issued with. Lewis's view was that the Bloody Sunday issue should be reopened so that the stain it had left on his regiment's reputation might be cleansed.

A variation of the same argument was expressed in a letter to Prime Minister Major from MPs Harry Barnes and Peter Bottomley, chairmen of the Labour and Tory backbench Northern Ireland Committees, urging an initiative to remove a grievance which they suggested was fuelling support for the IRA and delaying 'reconciliation'. Bottomley, a former Northern Ireland minister, returned to the subject in early 1993, calling on Mayhew to 'admit that the 14 should never have been shot'. Mayhew responded with the standard line that 'It would be unwise to reopen matters that have been the subject of a judicial inquiry, and to reopen these later I don't propose to do.' (It might not be fanciful to speculate that the awkwardness of the syntax reflected the beginnings of uncertainty as to whether the line on Bloody Sunday could be held much longer.)

The argument that reopening the Bloody Sunday issue could help hasten a resolution of the Northern problem on terms unharmful to British interests hardly coincided with the relatives' reasoning. But it added to pressure on the British authorities, and was to become steadily more persuasive as events moved towards the IRA ceasefire of 1994 and thence to the talks that culminated in the 1998 Belfast Agreement.

In 1994, campaigners and John Major executed another circuit of the old argument when the BSJC was instrumental in Belfast solicitors Madden & Finucane (M&F) writing formally to the Premier asking for a new inquiry. Major's undersecretary responded on 17 February along familiar lines. From the BSJC's point of view, one purpose of the exchange was to facilitate a new application to the European Court of Human Rights (ECHR) claiming a breach by the Ministry of Defence of the right to life provisions of Article Two of the European Convention. The ECHR lays down that applications must be lodged within six months of all domestic legal remedies being exhausted. M&F submitted the application on 17 August and tried to argue that the six months time limit should run from the 17 February refusal of a new inquiry. In April 1996, the 27-member Commission unanimously rejected this logic. However, the legal team that had worked on the application, most prominently Patricia Coyle, remained engaged on the issue. Until the announcement of the Saville Inquiry, M&F remained the only legal firm involved in Bloody Sunday, and formally represented all of the families and the wounded – although still not all family members were relating directly to the legal actions.

Others who had become involved in the European case, including Jane Winter of the human rights organisation British–Irish Rights Watch (BIRW), remained actively committed to the Bloody Sunday cause. A paper by Winter responding to the failure of the European initiative, *Bloody Sunday: Where Do We Go From Here?*, considered what options would be available if no new inquiry was conceded and other legal avenues remained closed. The paper suggested recruiting 'a whole range of international figures and bodies' to pressurise the British government and, if that failed, drawing on the same support to establish an unofficial inquiry 'under internationally-recognised figures'. Additionally, Winter suggested, a beginning might be made on establishing a permanent archive of Bloody Sunday material so that none of the accumulating expertise and information would be lost, and that a preliminary basis for establishing the truth would be in place for future use.

Winter's paper was one of a number of strategic plans, not all of them as clearly formulated, discussed and sometimes quarrelled over at BSJC gatherings. All options were time- and energy-consuming, and expensive. Although the Bloody Sunday case was fairly soon to be seen as a gravy train for lawyers – and some of the fees eventually earned by Inquiry lawyers, in the perspective of the families and the wounded, were truly fabulous – there was neither huge reward nor seeming prospect of it for Patricia Coyle and M&F in this period. The scepticism, even suspicion, of many in the profession towards the enterprise was clear in the response of the firm that had represented the families in the 1974 civil action to a request from M&F for access to the papers from that case for use in the European application.

'As you know,' wrote a representative of J. Christopher Napier and Co. of Belfast:

> each of these actions is barred by the Discharges signed. I therefore consider that you have not shown any lawful cause for wishing to copy the documents which I own, and that I am within my rights to refuse to allow ... What possible purpose could you and your clients now have in pursuing the 'Bloody Sunday Justice Campaign' after all this time? The letter from John Kelly, the Chair of the Bloody Sunday Justice Campaign, indicated that a claim against the Ministry of Defence is what is contemplated. How can such now possibly be brought?

True enough, the European case was to come to nothing. But it garnered continuing wide publicity and helped keep the issue simmering, particularly in Derry. The BSJC had learned to see every tangentially relevant development as a peg on which to hang a new intervention. There had been much satisfaction among the group in October 1993 when a lively media debate followed a flurry of statements from the BSJC and individual families greeting reports that detectives from Scotland Yard were to travel to Buenos Aires to investigate complaints that paratroopers had killed captured Argentine soldiers during the Falklands War more than ten years previously. Campaign spokesman Paul Doherty described the Falklands investigation as 'a clear precedent .... Bloody Sunday remains an issue which must be specifically dealt with by both Britain and Ireland.'

Irish governments too had begun to pay attention. University of Ulster law lecturer Angela Hegarty, a leading academic authority on Bloody Sunday, has suggested in an assessment of the Saville experience that intelligence gatherers sent North to listen to and report back on Nationalist feeling in the mid-1990s helped alert the Dublin authorities to growing interest in the issue. The BSJC began to find a readier welcome in Dublin than a few years earlier. What this mainly reflected was likely the fact that the nascent peace process involved the Dublin government taking on significant Northern issues which might otherwise become or remain the prerogative of still only slightly constitutional Republicans. The BSJC had succeeded in making Bloody Sunday one such issue. In 1995, Taoiseach John Bruton of Fine Gael, a vigorous opponent of Sinn Fein, designated a civil servant specifically to liase with the Bloody Sunday families and to keep the government abreast of developments.

The Irish Congress of Trade Unions (ICTU), too, came onside, agreeing at its biennial conference in Derry in 1994 to call for a new inquiry. Despite six of the dead having been union members, ICTU officialdom had hitherto been silent on the massacre, fearing that taking a stand might alienate Protestant members in the North: it is a moot point whether the attitude was more insulting to Protestant trade unionists or to the Bloody Sunday families. In fact, the North's largest union, Northern Ireland Public Service Alliance (NIPSA), prompted by the persistent campaigning of one of its Derry stalwarts, Eileen Webster, had endorsed the call for a new inquiry as far back as 1977 and annually reiterated its position. 'We just kept at it,' recalls Webster. 'It became something of a ritual.' NIPSA suffered no resignations as a result. The adoption by the wider movement of the NIPSA position was further indication that Bloody Sunday issue was moving in from the margins.

Meanwhile, assiduous digging began to unearth long-buried information. Jane Winter and Patricia Coyle discovered a series of telling documents in the Public Records Office in Kew. Faxed to the office at West End Park where the BSJC was now based, each became the occasion for another flurry of statements and outbreaks of lobbying. Deluging media outlets with suggested leads for new stories became a regular BSJC activity. One memo which made front-page headlines, sections of which were soon to be recited verbatim in Bogside pubs, recorded the meeting between Heath and Widgery on the day after the massacre, at which Widgery agreed to head the first Inquiry. The Premier was noted as counselling the judge to keep in mind that 'In Northern Ireland we are fighting not just a military war but also a propaganda war.' When he came to give evidence to Saville in January 2003, Heath seemed bewildered and outraged at suggestions that this statement was improper. (Heath seemed outraged at being required to answer questions about Bloody Sunday at all.)

In 1996, the BSJC handed to Don Mullan – a Derry writer who had marched as a teenager on Bloody Sunday and who was now widely known for involvement in issues affecting the 'third world' – a plastic bag discovered in a cupboard in the West End Park office stuffed with copies of the civilian statements gathered by NICRA in 1972 and ignored by Widgery. A number of the statements referred to shots fired on Bloody Sunday by soldiers other than paras from a stretch of the Derry Walls where they beetle over the Bogside. In *Eyewitness Bloody Sunday*, published the following year, Mullan argued that three of the dead may have been shot from the Walls and not by paratroopers at all. Although evidence at Saville was strongly to suggest that, actually, none of the casualties had been inflicted from the Walls, the statements constituted important new material: although obviously relevant, they hadn't been considered by Widgery. This significantly strengthened the legal, as opposed to the moral or political, case for a new inquiry, and brought on board elements which had hitherto shied away for fear of seeming association with an anti-state campaign without a respectable legal basis. Family members accompanied Mullan to Britain and the United States, pointing to the new evidence and finding a new audience.

Patricia Coyle drove a boot-load of documents, most of them recovered from Kew, to Limerick and passed them to law professor Dermot Walsh, who had been commissioned by the newly formed BST to produce an analysis of the material for submission to the two governments. (The BST, with an overlapping membership with the BSJC, had been founded in 1997 with a legal status that enabled it to access funds from major foundations unavailable to the BSJC. It was tasked to provide a range of services, and to realise Jane Winter's idea for a permanent Bloody Sunday archive: the Museum of Free Derry, located in Glenfada Park in a building still pockmarked with bullets from Bloody Sunday, is set to open in late 2005. During the Saville hearings, the BST maintained a centre for the families close to the Guildhall, provided a professional counselling service for family members, and employed John Kelly and Michael McKinney to liase with the Inquiry and, later, as administrator, Jean Hegarty, whose brother Kevin McElhinney, 17, had been shot in the back as he crawled along Rossville Street on his hands and knees.) Walsh's *The Bloody Sunday Tribunal of Inquiry: A Resounding Defeat for Truth, Justice and the Rule of Law* was published by the BST in 1997.

Meanwhile, Channel 4 News, in the persons of producer Lena Ferguson and reporter Alex Thomson, began compiling a series of reports including interviews with soldiers claiming to have fired from the Walls, alleging that command and control had broken down on the day and that 'shameful and disgraceful acts' had been committed. Channel 4 News also claimed that Widgery officials had deliberately changed the statement of at least one soldier so as to conceal army misbehaviour. On the strength of their Bloody Sunday reports, Ferguson and Thomson were to win the 1997 UK Home News Award from the Royal Television Society.

The success of the BSJC in moving the issue into the mainstream was reflected, too, in attacks by conservative commentators in Britain and Ireland uneasy at its potential to boost hostility towards state authority at a time of unpredictable change. Each occasion was an opportunity to air the issue and engender debate. In January 1997, *Irish Times* and *Sunday Telegraph* commentator Kevin Myers mounted, in the *Times*, a polemical onslaught against plans to mark the 25th anniversary with a weekend of theatre, concerts and debates, as well the march. Myers lambasted the 'aggressive self-pity' of the families in creating 'a degrading cult of victim hood (sic)' and orchestrating a 'festival of selective commemoration'. The families had facilitated 'Sinn Fein-IRA', he suggested, in using Bloody Sunday as an excuse for perpetrating subsequent atrocities.

Threatening action for libel, Peter Madden of M&F responded in terms which echoed the wider debate:

> The suggestion that the families 'should' publicly express a particular opinion at the attendance of members of Sinn Fein at any commemoration ... suggests that there is some moral imperative against which they may be judged and found wanting.

The *Irish Times* settled out of court. The substantial damages helped fund the campaign as it moved into its most decisive period.

In June 1997, the new Fianna Fail-led administration of Bertie Ahern presented the just-elected government of Tony Blair with a 178-page assessment of the new material, drawing on the Mullan and Walsh books, Channel 4 News and other media reports, and on a range of material from its own and other archives. The assessment had mainly been compiled by Eamonn McKee, the Department of Foreign Affairs official appointed by the previous administration to the Bloody Sunday desk. The bulk of the document comprised a paragraph-by-paragraph critique of the Widgery Report in the light of the new information. In a covering letter, Ahern told Blair that:

> Your predecessor had indicated that he would be glad to receive a copy of our Assessment and that he and his Government would look at it with an open mind .... I believe that your approach to this issue can help to remove a source of profound distress not only to the relatives but to the nationalist community generally.

The preface placed the issue squarely in the context of the developing peace process, and for the first time asserted the families' demand for a new inquiry as Irish Government policy. 'Given the status and currency which was accorded to the Widgery Report, the most appropriate and convincing redress would be a new Report, based on a new independent inquiry.' Bloody Sunday didn't figure in the talks under US Senator George Mitchell at Stormont Castle, which yielded the 'Good Friday Agreement', but it was an important issue between the governments in the context of the broader peace process.

In 1991, no main-party TD had turned up for the launch of the first book to call for a new inquiry. Six years later, in October 1997, a family delegation organised by the BSJC was welcomed to meetings successively with Ahern, Bruton, Labour Party leader Dick Spring, Democratic Left leader Proinsias De Rossa and the deputy leader of the Progressive Democrats, Bobby Molloy. Each competed with the others in the fervour with which they backed the families' case and their call for a new inquiry.

When Prime Minster Blair announced the new inquiry in the Commons on 29 January 1998, the families celebrated what they saw, accurately, as a victory for their campaign. But they were also aware that broader political developments had, at the least, facilitated their success. And some were anxious lest new political imperatives curtail the scope of the Inquiry or limit its findings. The announcement came ten weeks before the Stormont talks were to climax in the Agreement. Lord Saville was to make his first visit to Derry to deliver his opening statement in the Guildhall on 3 April, seven days before Good Friday.

The talk was of reconciliation and forgiveness, and of a new era of balance between 'the two communities'. In this context, the Bloody Sunday Inquiry could be seen (and was, by those so minded) as an achievement in which the Catholic/Nationalist community might rejoice and which Protestants/Unionists might accept, whether grudgingly or in a spirit of generosity, in the interests of the new accord. Logically enough in this perspective, anti-Agreement Unionists, led in Derry by Gregory Campbell of the Democratic Unionist Party, opposed the Inquiry outright and urged their supporters to see it as part-and-parcel of a wider sell-out of Protestant/Unionist interests. There was no substantial body of opinion to welcome the Inquiry as being in the interests of the citizenry as a whole, the entitlement of any who had suffered injustice for so long at the hands of the State.

The families were in the main optimistic. Most felt there was reason to believe Blair's concession of the Inquiry might foreshadow a more open British approach to Bloody Sunday generally, including by the military.

Saville's remit was wider than Widgery's and referred specifically to evidence that Widgery hadn't considered: 'To inquire into the events of Sunday, 30 January 1972 which led to loss of life in connection with the procession in Londonderry on that day, taking account of any new information relevant to events on that day.'

The BBC marked the announcement of the Inquiry by re-showing the 1992 documentary, *Remember Bloody Sunday*, in which the Commander of the First Paras, Lt. Col. Derek Wilford, had declared that 'I don't believe my soldiers were wrong.' Asked whether the victims could be considered innocent, he had replied: 'Oh no. I can't believe that. That would be to believe that my soldiers were wrong.'

However, in a contemporary interview screened the same weekend, Wilford seemed to sing from an updated song sheet: 'One cannot help thinking we were taken there to teach them a lesson, to go in knocking a few heads and show them they cannot have a no-go area.' Ultimate responsibility for the shooting, he suggested, lay not with military but political leaders. The plan 'has to come from higher than the brigade commander. The germ of it must have started in London.'

But hopes that pressure from the Inquiry and a need to displace blame would prompt the soldiers to come clean and burst the dam of deceit that Jackson had begun to construct back in 1972 were soon to fade.

The families' early optimism was initially heightened by rulings from

Saville in December 1998 that the soldiers should testify at the Guildhall and under their own names. Even then, however, the sceptical noted that the wording wasn't water-tight: 'All who are called to give oral evidence should expect to give their evidence in the Derry Guildhall .... Anonymity ... will not be granted automatically.'

Perhaps encouraged by the initial hint of equivocation in the rulings, the soldiers challenged both of them in the courts. In July 1999, the Court of Appeal in London ruled that for reasons of their safety the soldiers' names should be withheld. In December 2001, the Appeal Court ordered, again on grounds of safety, that the soldiers should not be compelled to testify in Derry. As a result, all soldiers other than a very few whose names were already in the public domain were to testify under cipher at hearings in Methodist Central Hall, Westminster, between September 2002 and October 2003. Politicians including Heath, civil servants and intelligence officers also gave their evidence at Central Hall (as did one Derry witness, former Provisional IRA man Paddy Ward, whose account of IRA activity on the day, and of his own feats of derring-do, incited both derision and anger among the families). Arrangements sanctioned by Saville to protect some witnesses' identities left little to chance: a video screen in the hall was concealed from public view during the testimony of one unnamed ex-intelligence officer giving evidence via videolink from a secret location outside the UK.

The Inquiry went to considerable trouble to help family members attend the London hearings. Praise for Inquiry officials involved in the London phase of the operation was unstinting. Nevertheless, the move was hugely disruptive, and greatly resented. All family members believed that the venue change and arrangements for ensuring anonymity – as well as subsequent use of Public Interest Immunity certificates (PIIs) to block the emergence of intelligence information – had compromised the public character of the Inquiry. There was considerable debate as to whether Saville had been thwarted by the English courts in his desire for openness, or had made his rulings in contented expectation of their being set aside.

The number of family members attending London hearings varied from week to week from a dozen to more than a hundred, depending on what evidence was scheduled. The usual itinerary had the group travelling to London on Sunday afternoon, staying for four nights in a Pimlico hotel within walking distance of Westminster, and returning to Derry on Thursday evening. For some, on occasion, there was an element of adventure, even holiday, in the experience. For most of the families most of the time, however, it was an onerous imposition. Family lives were damaged. But 'there can't be a word spoken that we aren't there to hear', explained

Damien Donaghey, 16 when wounded by a sniper as he stood on waste ground by William Street.

In all, the Inquiry was to sit for 434 days. Oral hearings began in Derry Guildhall on 27 March 2000, with the opening address of Inquiry Chief Counsel Christopher Clarke. The first witness was heard on 28 November 2000. In all, 912 witnesses were to take the stand: 505 civilians, 245 soldiers, 33 police officers, nine forensic experts, 34 IRA members, 39 politicians, civil servants and intelligence officers, 49 journalists and seven priests. Clarke made his closing speech on 22 and 23 November 2004. Sixteen million words were spoken. A further 25 million words were logged in statements of 1,555 witnesses not called to the stand and in documents and records gathered by the Inquiry.

It is understood at the time of writing that the Report of the Inquiry will be published early in 2006.

For the families, living through the Inquiry was always emotional, frequently fraught, sometimes fascinating. And tedious, too, at times. None regrets the experience. All are relieved it is over. On 26 March 2000, the night before hearings began, as the families walked with supporters in a torch-lit procession from the monument in Rossville Street out from the Bogside and into Guildhall Square, Geraldine Doherty, niece of Gerald Donaghey, 17 when shot dead as he edged out from cover in Abbey Park, remarked to no one in particular, 'Now comes the hard part, thank God.'

1 Campaign

GERALDINE DOHERTY

I don't remember Bloody Sunday. I wasn't born. But I can remember from my very early days my mother talking about Gerald, ordering a wreath around January time and saying, 'It's for your Uncle Gerald.' I suppose I was about eight when I started going down to the memorial with my mum on the anniversary morning. It was always raining. Sometimes the priest would come, sometimes it would just have been the families and we would stand around and say the rosary and then talk for a bit and go home.

When I started being allowed to go on the marches, I was always at the front, me or my mum carrying the photo of Gerald. I always walked along not looking at people, but just holding the photo in front of me. I felt proud. I felt he was looking down, looking after me.

After a while, I asked questions about him: who he was, what he was like, who he hung around with, what he did. I looked at all the photos of him. I still always see him in the denim jacket and trousers that he was killed in.

I never realised how bad Bloody Sunday was until I saw the TV film. My mum told me but I didn't realise. She was looking out from the flat and she said all she could see was the people's feet hitting the ground running, and then she heard the shouts and the screams. She was living in Rossville Street at the time, above the undertakers.

By the time I was 18 or 19, the families were getting together and I started going to the meetings, every Tuesday night up in West End Park. I really enjoyed sitting around with my mum and the other families, trying to work out how to get a new inquiry, organising to go around doors with a petition, thinking up protests. There would have been Micky McKinney, John Kelly, George Downey, Eileen Doherty, Tony Doherty, Banty and Linda Nash, and me and my mum. That would have been nearly it. The biggest reason for going would have been to give my

Geraldine Doherty, 31 (left), is a niece of Gerald Donaghey (above, left), aged 17 when shot dead as he ran from the paras in Abbey Park. Geraldine Doherty is single, a shop worker and lives in the Waterside area of Derry.

mum support, because she was on her own. But the more I went the more I got to know and the more interested I was.

I was shocked when Derry people didn't support us. I remember a woman at one door saying to me, 'Get away you murdering Bs, youse killed my son.' She thought we were the IRA. We had doors slammed in our face and people turning away and telling us it was a hopeless case. But I turned my feet and walked on to the next door. I ignored the bad and battered on.

Then Patricia Coyle came on board. She was with Madden & Finucane at the time. We put everything we had together and she took it all away and sorted it out. I remember thinking at that that there was hope. And I remember us all being called to a hotel about a film that was being made, and I thought, 'This is good, this is really hopeful, this is going somewhere.' That's the way we went on.

It was the same hotel, the Trinity on Strand Road, that we were called to and given what Tony Blair was going to say in the House of Commons agreeing to the Inquiry. We got that before he made the announcement. We all went out and marched up the Strand Road into the Guildhall Square to let the people of Derry know that it had happened, that we'd got the Inquiry.

JOHN KELLY

The families met once a year at the commemoration and went away again. We didn't know each other. I knew very little about the other families until the campaign began. Then people became close and started recalling stories of Bloody Sunday. Every family has a story, but in reality they're all the same. They all carried the same pain. I wasn't even in the room when I was elected chairman of the campaign. I went a message and when I came back I was chairman. I accepted because it was doing something for Mickey, for my mother, for my father and all the family and all the other families.

I had never had the experience of even chairing a meeting before. I wouldn't have known if I was doing the right thing. But I always remembered, and I still do, to say a prayer beforehand – 'Mickey, give me the strength to get through this, and make sure it will work out OK.' Before I go out to a meeting I've looked at a painting of Mickey which I have in the house, 32 years old, painted by Jimmy McCartney, an old man who lived in Bloomfield. I would look and see whether he's smiling at me, and I'd say, 'Are we going to do all right today?'

I'm not a religious person – I would go to mass now and again – but I think that wee bit of prayer helped me to get through all the difficulties, all the problems that arose with directions we were going in. Maybe other families did the same thing. I don't know.

Maybe I didn't look after him well enough that day. I remember speaking to him before the march and saying, 'Look if anything happens get off sides,' realising that he never took part in a march before in his life, never took part in a riot. He was training to be a sewing machine mechanic and spent most of the week in Belfast at the Tech. He came home on Fridays, was going out with his girlfriend, rearing his pigeons, then going back to Belfast on Sunday night. So he had no time. Plus he had no interest in politics at all. I had no interest in politics. I took part in the marches but I wasn't a political thinker. I suppose it turned into a debt: 'He ain't heavy, he's my brother'. I'm carrying Mickey and trying to achieve something for him.

The first meeting we had was in Pilot's Row. We had tried it before three or four times, but nothing came out of it. I don't know what it was then, maybe a spark from the 20th anniversary. I looked around me and saw a lot of individuals – there were 30 or 40 there – and I said to myself, 'Maybe there is a chance this time.' Then we had a formal meeting in the

Pat Finucane Centre and sat down and elected officers. There were 10 or 15 at that.

One of the reasons it worked was that everybody had involvement, not just certain people. We met every Tuesday night, hail rain or snow, apart from Christmas. I always looked forward to those meetings, because we had a task to achieve, even if we didn't know how we were going to do it. It was ordinary people doing this thing together. I'm a toolmaker by trade, Tony Doherty is a joiner, Mickey is a butcher, Gerry Duddy is a plasterer, and Linda, Mary Doherty and Geraldine were housewives. I have always felt those campaigning days were the best days. We bounced off one another. 'Let's go to Dublin, Prince Charlie's in Dublin, let's protest against him.' Going to see the four leaders of the main churches, approaching politicians, John Hume, Derry City Council, whoever we could think of. We realised we were going to have our ups and downs, but we were going to get on with it. At times, you felt really down. People you thought would come on board backed away. A lot of people thought we were Republicans, Sinn Feiners and all that sort of stuff. We have had to break down barriers and say, 'Look, I have my personal views, but I'm not here as a Shinner or an SDLP man or whatever, I'm the brother of some-one who was murdered on Bloody Sunday.' We had to work on that for a long time. And I remember somebody coming to me and saying, 'I wonder can you help me, I've a daughter who's looking for a flat, can you do anything for her?' Jesus, Missus …

You had your laughs, and you had your anger when people ignored you. But I enjoyed those days. I always made sure I was free for the meet-ings. Even my wife would say, 'Are you not going to the meeting?' I enjoyed looking around to see who would turn up and then getting the minutes out. I remember sitting at the Inquiry and somebody saying, 'Ah, I wish we could get back to the campaign days,' and I said, 'Aye.'

It was a lot of work, too. We travelled everywhere, met a lot of people. We went to England, travelled to America, Capitol Hill and the White House. That was after Don Mullan came on board. He wrote the book. We got great success from it. It was Don who mainly organised for us to go to America to lobby. We went to Boston, the coldest place I've ever felt in my life. The families then marched in the St Patrick's Day parade in New York. It was the AOH [Ancient Order of Hibernians] that looked after us.

The point of the book was to spread the word and to try and pull on board as many as we could. But we had the likes of the President of Ireland, Mary Robinson, who refused to meet the families, although eventually she did agree to meet some. A few of us said to tell her to stick her invitation up her arse.

John Kelly (left) was one of 12 children of a family from the Creggan Estate. Twenty-three on Bloody Sunday, he was six years older than Michael (right), a trainee sewing machine mechanic, who was shot dead at the Rossville Street barricade. Now married with six children, John Kelly works full-time for the Bloody Sunday Trust.

When things developed into the bigger group, different viewpoints and disagreements could creep in, and animosity as well. I found that very annoying because this wasn't about us, but about our Mickey and Gerry McKinney, Paddy Doherty, Jim Wray, Mickey Bridge and so on. It was easy for people with the best will in the world to lose sight of that. At times I had to re-address things, I'd say, 'What the fuck is going on here?' But we are still together, I don't look upon it as the Bloody Sunday families, it's the Bloody Sunday Family, maybe strained at times, but still together. We had our difficulties, but remain strong and determined in our quest for truth and justice.

EILEEN GREEN

Tony was nine when his father was murdered. He was 18 when he went to prison for four years. So he was 22 when he came out in 1985 and started talking about Bloody Sunday.

I was working in the shirt factory at the time and I remember him saying one day, 'Do the women you work with ever talk about Bloody Sunday? Do they think the Brits have just got away with it?' A while later, he talked to me about whether we could get the families together and find out their thoughts on what could be done. I helped him to get addresses. I knew where Ida McKinney lived, and Betty Walker, and a couple of the others. Then Tony got the Sinn Fein centre in Cable Street for a meeting. I remember Betty Walker and her mother and Mary Donaghy, plus Mr Wray and Mr Kelly, and myself and Tony. I think that was the first meeting. That's how we started.

Then we thought maybe we would get more people meeting somewhere else. Some people that might have felt a bit intimidated in a Sinn Fein office. So we got a place in Sackville Street, and it just built up from there. We didn't have a name at that point.

Sinn Fein had kept the march going from the second or third anniversary, but as things began to move on Tony said he'd ask Sinn Fein to let the families do the march, which they did. With the changeover, it all broadened out. It went from a few hundred every year to thousands.

I think one of the reasons Tony took on that role was that his father was his hero. He must have been thinking a lot on it when he was inside. By the time he came out, he was determined. He never got sidetracked. He was serious. Something would come up and you'd ask him and he'd say, 'I need a day to think about that.' Then he'd come back to you.

At that time, Tony didn't have a job. He worked away on Bloody Sunday all the time. He was a great analyser. We would get a letter from John Major and Tony would say, 'Don't think this means what it looks like, because here is what he's really saying.' I was working full time and I had the other children, but anything that Tony asked me to do, I did it.

Starting to make a weekend of the anniversary was a big step forward for us all. It was important to set up the Bloody Sunday lecture. Those were the best Friday nights I ever had. You think you know everything about Bloody Sunday because you have thought about it so much for so

Eileen Greene, 60 (right), a former factory worker, a mother of six, was married to Patrick Doherty, 31 (left, with her), a process worker with Du Pont, who was shot dead from behind as he crawled away from the soldiers at Joseph Place. Now married to Patrick Green, she lives in the Carnhill area.

long. But when you hear it put together from different points of view, then you see it all on a better background. Tony worked to make sure the lecture was right, that everybody who went could learn something from it. It all helped us deal with whatever came at us from any direction.

I think the first day I really started believing was the day Tony Blair was elected. Coming up to that election, I wasn't well. I was in the house all the time and I watched all the coverage. I would be interested in stuff like that anyway. I remember seeing him with his own family and it just clicked in me that here was a guy who might listen. I remembered Archbishop Makarios of Cyprus. He was arrested and exiled to the Seychelles for supporting independence. It took a change to a Labour government to turn things around and have Makarios brought back home. I had that in my head. That was the first time I ever said to people that I thought we were actually going to get the Inquiry. Blair seemed an honest man with family feelings that we could get through to. Of course, I am not talking about Tony Blair now. I am talking about Tony Blair then.

The night it was announced we were all in the Trinity Hotel. I just cried. We had been on the road so long and now the word of a lord chief justice was being overturned. History was being overturned.

The only politicians actually interested from the start were Sinn Fein. Every time they were in 10 Downing Street, Bloody Sunday was mentioned. I think there were other politicians who did become interested once we had the Inquiry but, I mean, it was too late then.

JIMMY DUDDY

All the families were very open minded in the beginning. There were differences, all right. But then they found that a space developed so that everybody could be courteous enough, even if they weren't friends. The common objective was the gel that kept everybody together. My father had been doing a great job from the start representing my uncle. I felt a certain amount of envy of the bond the families had developed before I came in at the time the Inquiry started.

We were lucky in the sense that Johnny died a couple of months after Bloody Sunday. Although it was tragic and hard for us to watch him go, we were the lucky ones of the 14 families. The other 13 didn't get to say goodbye. It was hard to see a 59-year-old man fade away so quickly. He always reminded me of Tommy Cooper. He had that presence about him, a jolly big man. That's how I remember him. That's the picture I kept in my mind as we worked towards the Inquiry.

Compared to the ten of the victims under 20, so you could say that a 59-year-old had had a good life. That shielded us to a certain degree. But the grief was still the same. Johnny and Margaret had no children of their own and were a big part of my family's life. Over the years, some members of some other families had nervous breakdowns. A lot of people had to help each other through to come out the other end. That's how the real bond developed.

I think Blair became prime minister with a lot of things on his mind that he wanted to put right and the Bloody Sunday action was one of them. He announced the Inquiry and that brought great joy. But then the Brits brought all these law cases that had to be fought. The British establishment and military were always trying to change the boundaries and the goal posts. We'd got the Inquiry, but now they wanted to get it their own way. All throughout, they were to show that they wanted it narrower and narrower.

BERNARD GILMOUR

I was at the very start of the campaign. We went everywhere. Meetings were steady, every Tuesday or Wednesday, and contacts with the Irish Government, etc. were regular. That went on for seven years before Blair agreed to an inquiry. We elected individuals to speak for us, John Kelly and Mickey Bridge, for example. They weren't to think of themselves as any better than us. They were doing this for us and that was it.

I don't think I thought about it much in political terms until the hearings started. My feeling was more basic. Everybody in Derry felt with the families. You would see it during the marches, the way we'd be recognised. Everybody knew sooner or later something would have to be done.

TERESA McGOWAN

My husband was wounded. The families that had people murdered were maybe feeling far worse than I was. Some of them had been working in it long before we came into it. When we did join in, I saw people I knew – if not the person themselves, I knew their mothers, fathers, families. It amazed me. You just heard about the 'Bloody Sunday Families', but when I realised I knew them actually as families, it really was a shock. How could all this have gone on and me not know who they were? Of course, we hadn't been involved.

Danny never went back to work after Bloody Sunday, and I was out working. He was glad when the Inquiry was announced but he always thought it would be another Widgery. I attended the hearings for Danny. It amazed me how some of the others had learned so much about it. It was mainly through talking to them that I gained my knowledge. They were powerful, those people. They never gave in; never let their loved ones down. It opened my eyes to things I can't explain. Danny, he just wanted it all blocked out of his mind. Danny was very protective of his family. If he came in, he would ask where they all were. He questioned them, used to wait at night for them to come in. He'd say, 'Don't you go down there, don't get involved, don't know nothing.'

I always came down to the meetings. I used to feel so thick sitting in and not being able to speak up but I knew there were plenty who were in it heart and soul and knew what they were talking about. I thought to myself, 'How do they keep all that in their heads, how do they remember it?'

I remember the day the news came through on the TV. We were all in the Rathmor Centre, waiting on some kind of word. It was fantastic, a vindication of all the effort. I didn't have much part in it, but I thought, 'Thank god for people who can stand it and stick it and go on and on.'

MAURA YOUNG

F or a long time I didn't know very much about Bloody Sunday. John was the youngest and I was next to him. My older brothers tried to shield me from it. They dealt with everything. So the campaign was well under way by the time I became involved, which I suppose was around the mid-1990s. It was when a petition was being taken to London. I suppose there were about five families active at that stage. Then they announced the Inquiry, we all needed solicitors, and everybody weighed in and came together. Everybody had their own ideas. I wouldn't say there were rows then, but there were disagreements, same as anything where there's a whole lot of people. So many want to be leaders, so many don't, you are bound to get a clash of personalities. But at the end of the day we were all fighting for the same thing.

LIAM WRAY

O riginally, there were the simple demands of the campaign. But as it went on, it became obvious that the families were not unified. They had different political objectives and different ideas as to a resolution.

The main demand was that those responsible for Bloody Sunday should be prosecuted. By the time the Inquiry started, there were, I felt, some that were moving away from that demand. They would have been listening to people who had that political view, not focusing on what should have been a human rights issue, to be dealt with apolitically rather than orchestrated to suit what was happening in the peace process and within particular political parties. Our family was very cautious at that time.

Madden & Finucane were working with the families of the 14 who lost their lives and at least 13 of the wounded. It was nothing personal, but I wasn't happy with the way Peter Madden wanted to conduct the case. Maybe he just wanted to make the thing a bit more manageable. At one stage, he declared that he would provide information on a 'need to know' basis. Our family believed that the solicitor was there to follow our instructions. When we went to bed at night we needed to know that if we didn't get the result we deserved, at least we had done the best we could and could sleep with an easy conscience.

All the families had the same feeling of grief, anger and frustration. But some wouldn't want to spend the hours looking at the legal complexities. As lay people, it is very difficult. All some wanted was the names of their relatives cleared. Others wanted the soldiers hanged. With one legal team it was going to be difficult to have your voice represented the distinct way you wanted.

Bloody Sunday was not just about the soldiers but about a government decision that Derry people should learn a lesson. There was an attitude within the military in 1972 that if they broke Derry, they would have imposed control on the civil rights movement. It was important for our family that that political aspect was followed to the limit. The Bloody Sunday operation had the knowledge of the British prime minister, the home secretary, the chief of the general staff. They set the mechanisms in place that led to the events.

So, shortly after he made his opening statement, which didn't encompass all that, we sent a letter to Lord Saville saying:

> I, Liam Wray, on behalf of the Wray family, whose brother Jim was murdered by British paratroops on Sunday 30 January '72, since known as Bloody Sunday, and whose reputation was tarnished by Lord Widgery at his Tribunal in '72, would like to inform you that we have no confidence in the Inquiry that you presently chair.

We withdrew just four months after the Inquiry's inauguration. So our family was out in the cold. It might sound strange but this was the first time in six or seven years there was a bit of relaxation.

There were lots of hurts that developed. When our family left, there were people saying we were breaking the ranks or whatever. There was a sort of a moral blackmail at times.

We came back in with our own legal representation around October the same year. I think one of Peter's team mentioned our Jim's name, and we thought we aren't in the Inquiry, we don't want Jim's name even mentioned. So I went to another solicitor. Basically, he said that the Inquiry had been set up by Parliament to investigate Bloody Sunday, and that if we weren't there Jim's death would be investigated anyway, and his interests represented by others. He suggested going in and fighting our corner, and indicated he would love to take part. He said 'My commitment is: I will tell you my opinion and I give you my advice but at the end of the day I will follow your instruction.' That was the sort of person we were looking for.

At the start, Saville wanted only three solicitors, three barristers and three QCs. The Madden team managed to up that to five solicitors, five barristers and five QCs. I said we are not going back without our own solicitor, own barrister, own QC. Also, at that point there were no Derry solicitors within the Inquiry. Peter and most of his team were Belfast-based.

So the family discussed it and instructed our solicitor, Greg McCartney, to write to the Inquiry explaining why we were coming back in but that we wanted separate representation. This did cause a problem between families. Some thought, 'Who do they think they are?'

Then, the McGuigan family and the Nash family, and two of the wounded, Bridge and Bradley, got their own representation.

In hindsight, I think it was the best thing that happened. With different legal teams, there was a self-generating competitiveness. They had to be better than they would normally be.

Our legal team focused a lot on the political responsibilities for Bloody Sunday. That did cause friction. There was an element of, 'I only give a fuck about me.' Maybe barristers or solicitors were saying to their particular clients, 'You don't worry about anybody else, we are your team.'

There were some horrendous Bloody Sunday meetings, things said and done and individuals attacked in a despicable way. We all started off behind the same three demands. But we were going through a peace process, talk of prisoners being released, people out after three years of a life sentence, paramilitaries on the run coming back. Some found the demand for prosecution not acceptable to their own political agenda.

The Inquiry was part of a deal to do with the peace process. When it was announced, we wouldn't have seen that. Maybe we have big egos. We felt we had achieved something ourselves. But the truth was, deals were done as part of the peace process and that's the main reason there was an inquiry.

I believe that those same political considerations have dictated the parameters and the nature of the inquiry and what the basic conclusions will be, whereas the event should have been investigated as an independent happening, with everything open to scrutiny. I also think that some political parties which had been pushing Blair for an Inquiry would be quite happy with a sanitised version of Bloody Sunday events now, because they don't want extra problems created for the peace process.

You never have ownership. Once you walk into the Guildhall or Central Hall you know you don't have ownership. I looked at the Inquiry as a pendulum at rest dead centre, and I believed that the best we could do was push it slightly one way and prevent it from slightly going the other. It took all of our efforts to push it towards the side of truth. We were never going to get it to go full swing.

MICHAEL McKINNEY

When the campaign started, there were six or eight people actively involved. Then the Inquiry loomed, other families came in, and major differences started.

At the start, everybody agreed to leave our politics outside. But some people had problems with one individual because he was politically involved. There were differences beginning to fester. At one point, I was going for chair and I passed a remark to this individual about voting for me. He went and told a couple of others and the whole fury started. Things started to splinter. It was a very bad, awkward time.

It seemed to me that people were looking for that bit of power, although, really, there was no power involved.

I struggled to chair meetings. I was being badgered all the time. There were times I couldn't even get the meeting started. It was through these differences that some people left Madden & Finucane.

Some people say that the Inquiry started because of the peace process. I wouldn't like to think that. Bloody Sunday sits on its own. I was told by somebody in Dublin that there were civil servants on their knees begging Tony Blair not to open this Inquiry. But by the time he came in, looking back, we had the case made. When I think of the campaign now, I think of half a dozen people sitting around a table in an office in West End Park on Tuesday nights. That was the foundation of the whole thing. Once the Inquiry was set up, there was a tidal wave of people becoming involved. That's when the main rows started. I'm conscious that a lot of what happened before that is almost forgotten. There were quiet nights in West End Park when we were saying that we would have to go to Dublin or London, but we didn't know how. I remember we took 13 people down to Dublin for some publicity thing. With hiring a minibus and food and everything it cost almost £500, which had to come from somewhere. The first time we went to London was to push the case to the European Court of Human Rights. That took money. We became aware of the reality that we wouldn't get anywhere if we didn't have funds. That we did raise the money shows how much determination there was. If it hadn't been for that group from the families and other supporters on the circumference succeeding in doing that, the Inquiry would never have happened. Patricia Coyle did a lot of work at that time, too. She did an awful lot of work on her own in that period.

We held dances in the Delacroix Bar. One of the first cleared £73. A lot later, we had the Wolfe Tones in the Clanree and made £4,000 in one night. The trip to America, to New York, Boston and Washington, where we met senators and what have you, I think we got £800 from the Ancient Order of Hibernians locally for that. Then, on a yearly basis, when they came over from America for the march, they'd have a cheque for $1,000 or $2,000 for us. The AOH in Newry organised functions for us. The AOH in the campaign years was very generous to us.

Our first real contact with the British government came in 1997 when John Kelly and myself, and Don Mullan, Peter Madden and John Hume, went up to Stormont and met Patrick Mayhew, and handed him the new evidence. He said, 'OK, I'll take it away and look at it.' Very soon after that, the changeover to New Labour came and Mo Mowlam was secretary of state. Mo phoned John and said, 'OK, we are considering the new evidence, we'll set up a meeting.' I think that was the first time that they contacted us, instead of us lobbying them. We met her in London at the Northern Ireland Office, and she said, 'You won't be getting what you're looking for, but I feel you'll be happy with what you are getting.' We were looking for an international inquiry, with a British judge, an Irish judge and a judge from Africa or wherever. Of course, what we got were Commonwealth judges.

MICKEY BRIDGE

You can't take 28 different groups of people and expect them to all sing from the same hymn sheet. Everybody has their own opinions of what should happen. There are people who used the Inquiry and there are people who, in my opinion, abused it.

There used to be regular discussions between the whole collective, though there were certain families who attended and families who didn't. Discussion deteriorated a bit over time, because of differences in approach rather than anything else. John Kelly and I tried to get a coordinated approach to it. Sometimes he disagreed, sometimes I disagreed. Sometimes he ignored me, sometimes I ignored him.

I think the Inquiry came about because the Public Records Office was being thrown open under the 30-year rule and the Irish government was threatening to publish what they deemed to be the facts. That's taking nothing away from those who lobbied and brought the campaign to the British politicians, or from the British politicians that campaigned for it. But if the British authorities could have withheld the documents, the Inquiry would never have happened. It was a political move to control the evidence.

JEAN HEGARTY

I lived in Canada for a long time, so I wasn't involved in Bloody Sunday as an issue. I never had any guilt about that in itself, but when I got back here in 1995, I felt maybe I had neglected my mother and father's needs, that now was the time. So I got involved.

Because, I'd lived away, I always kind of wondered … Kevin was 14 when I left, so I didn't really know what he was at or what he was like when he was 17. I always wondered what the circumstances were. Then there was a terrible incident with the Canadian Army in Somalia, when a teenager was tortured to death in a compound. People were just horrified that their own people could do that sort of thing. That was in 1993. Before, I would have been one of those people who, when the authorities said something, would have accepted it. That was the first time that I began to have doubts. That built in me. It was the beginning of my questioning, of believing that maybe things were not as they seemed. I came back in 1995, when the campaign was already under way. Our family hadn't really been involved prior to that.

I was married to a fellow from Creggan. He had worked in the BSR factory on Bligh's Lane making record players. It closed down in 1967. We were married and left here on the same day for Canada, and lived in Toronto. We were economic migrants; we went on an assisted passage. My family was from Pennyburn. Listening to me and listening to Hugo, you'd have thought we grew up in two different towns. My memories of the RUC would have been of a big cop taking us for sleigh rides down the Duncreggan Road. There was the police station at the top of the Grosvenor Road with just two young constables in it.

I was the eldest of five children. Kevin was the middle child. He was 14 when I went away, 17 on Bloody Sunday. So I did have questions. What was Kevin in 1972? All sorts of things could have changed. I wouldn't have views against the Brits or against the soldiers or anything like that. But I hold that against them, that they put doubts in my mind.

I came home for Kevin's funeral. When I went back, people would ask me, 'Your brother was killed in the Troubles, what was it about?' And I would answer, 'He was the teenage brother I didn't really know.' I would say, 'My parents believe he wasn't involved in anything.' But I knew lots of parents would have believed their sons weren't involved in anything.

My memories of Kevin would have been as a big sister. I was five years older. He was quiet and shy and I was a bully. I have memories of a pesky kid getting in my way when I was courting in the sitting room. He had had a turn in his eye when he was a child, and would have been shy and self-conscious. I couldn't picture him in another way. I think in many ways that difference in my memory helped me to cope with his death, because that person in the coffin wasn't Kevin. That was the teenager I didn't know.

Afterwards, I would have phoned my mammy on his birthday and his anniversary. But even though my own daughter was four in 1972, I had no conception of a mother losing a child, what it would do. I have a fair bit of guilt about turning my back, walking away, especially since I was the eldest. Being back now, that's something that really distresses me. One of my grandmothers lived until she was 94, but my uncle died much earlier, and she always said that it disturbed the natural order of things, a child dying before its parents, that it wasn't right. That sentence stays in my mind. I have no conscious memory of being selfish in getting on with my life, but in retrospect that's exactly what it was. The Troubles were here and I was there, and I had my own family. That's part of the reason I became involved in the campaign when I came back.

I discovered that different families in the campaign had different views, so there was always the possibility of conflict. There was a diverse range of things people wanted from the Inquiry – in terms of prosecutions of soldiers, and so on. I think that the expectations may have changed somewhat; that some people have mellowed. I'm fairly liberal about it, myself. I don't expect prosecutions, especially in view of the peace process. I'd like to see it, but I'm realistic.

JOHNNY CAMPBELL

I wouldn't doubt there was politics involved in setting up the tribunal, but that had nothing to do with us. Our family just wanted the truth of what happened to my father and all the rest. To me, it was a personal issue. The politics could look after themselves.

The family meetings at the early stage could involve a bit of debate and wheeling and dealing, right enough. But things got sorted and we got on with it. It didn't worry me. Sometimes you went in with an idea in your head and somebody would want to go a different road and you might say, 'Well, maybe that's a better idea than what I was thinking.'

I would rather we had all stayed with a single legal team. We should have gone the whole hog together, come what may. But there it is, people will always have different opinions. I never had any bother with Madden & Finucane, and I never had any bother with the families' group or committees or anything. I had no complaints.

KATE AND PATRICK NASH

K*ate:* As a family, we weren't participating in the campaign when the Bloody Sunday office opened. We felt that this group was going to hassle the people of Derry for money to set up their office and things like that. I've certainly had a change of heart, although, even now, not all our family would be supportive of the Bloody Sunday Trust.

When the Inquiry was announced, the group had to split because it was every man for himself. This was the final opportunity for the families to have the truth known about their particular relative, so you had to go and get the best possible person. You will never see another inquiry into this.

P*atrick:* The fact that the families had fought for the Inquiry did give a sense of ownership when it at last came about. Going to meetings, talking about it, planning, just keeping on chipping away, they did that for years. I played no part in that. Achieving the Inquiry was a vindication of other people's efforts. They even managed to put pressure on the international community.

We never asked for an inquiry. We asked for the truth. But when it was announced, we went along with it. I personally thought it would be another Widgery, that they'd come in and say, 'Well, if the civil rights marchers hadn't come out on the street, the army wouldn't have gone in.' That was the sort of thing that I was expecting. I certainly wasn't expecting the length of time and the number of witnesses.

PATSY McDAID

I t was a shock when the Brits finally came out and said, 'You're getting your inquiry.' The Brits do things like that to put you off balance.

I think that when it was announced, the families should have taken more time. Within a couple of hours, the word was, 'This is great.' We'd waited 30 years. We should have taken a couple of days and mulled it over. We'd been fighting for an independent international inquiry. We never got that. Maybe we were never going to get it, but we should have let the Brits stew for a while, put our objections on paper and given it to them. That would have been a more strategic approach.

I was just a bit dodgy about it. I never had any great faith in it. You can see how they tried to drag it out as long as they could. The Brits are famous for doing things like that. Your doubts increase over time. After all, we know what happened and they know what happened.

The Brits did things throughout the world and it was all covered up through the years. But they didn't know how determined people here were. The Irish are a different people. If we are right, we'll go right through with whatever it takes. We must be the first in the world for the Brits to give another inquiry.

This was a hot potato for them and they were hoping for years that it would go away but it never did. For the first number of years, the English papers slagged everything that was happening. They played up that the IRA was involved, to try to discredit the people. But it backfired on them. Thousands of people marched on every Bloody Sunday commemoration because we were right and the Brits were wrong, and in the end we got another inquiry.

CAROLINE O'DONNELL

A fter my daddy was shot, he buried it. He never talked about it again. It was only when the Inquiry came up that I became really interested. I wouldn't have been at a lot of the meetings prior to that. So I was only starting to get to know the families when I started going to the Inquiry. I know that there was aggro among the families but I never got involved. I thought it was very sad. Bloody Sunday had brought everybody together, but they all had their own upbringing, their own families, their own values and beliefs, so there were bound to be differences.

I thought it was fantastic what the original group had achieved. Kay, Mickey, John and so on, they went through huge emotional pain, lobbying, pleading, publicising, getting doors shut in their faces, being told it could never happen, but they did it in the end.

There were differences of opinion over things like strategy. The media – there would always have been problems there. When there were statements put out, somebody would say that everybody should have been consulted. 'Who are you to speak for me?' But even though there were differences, there was respect because, at the end of the day, everybody was after the one thing.

ALANA BURKE

Some maybe thought that one legal team couldn't give each of the dead and wounded the representation they needed. And I think there were personality clashes. It wasn't nice at the time, but everyone's entitled to whoever they want to represent them.

When the Inquiry was announced, I think the first reaction was, 'We're going to get these boys in the end up', that at long last everybody's story was going to be listened to, every wee detail, everything that was important. Whereas before, the surface wasn't even scratched. Fourteen people killed and 14 injured and it all just pushed to the side. Now, everybody was asking, 'Well, what do you want out of it, and what do you think you're going to get out of it?'

KEVIN McDAID

Over the years, our family never talked about it. After the anniversary marches, we would all go back to the house, for tea or whatever, and there would be discussion about the crowd or the speakers who were on that year. But we didn't talk of the actual event. Bloody Sunday killed my mother and father, my mother in particular. Her life changed big time when Michael was killed. Afterwards, she was never my mother as I knew her. She was never a happy person again. My father, too. We did everything we could for them as a family. As we got married we all would come back to the house with our children. It affected us all. We knew from that day on that my mother's attitude to life had changed. She lost a lot of her feeling inside.

There were other families with the same loss. It affected a great number of people. It affected the whole town. It's a big thing in our lives and it will be until such times as we get what we are looking for, if we ever do.

As a family, we were never political, but we never lost sight of Bloody Sunday. From day one, we all had our own children out every year on the marches, and still do. As far as the campaign was concerned, for a long time that was really down to the likes of Mickey McKinney, John Kelly, Tony Doherty. It was when things came together in 1996 or 1997 that we became involved. We had a family meeting and it landed with me to become involved and do whatever had to be done.

When we heard that the Inquiry had been granted we were sceptical, and still are. Some of our family didn't want to be involved in any way whatsoever. But at the end of the day it was going to go ahead anyway, whether we were involved or not, so a majority decided we would go along with it. Of course, it was still in the back of everybody's mind that it was a British inquiry and might not work.

2 Saville

JEAN HEGARTY

My opinion of Saville changed over time. At the beginning I didn't know what to make of him, and then my confidence grew. But I think towards the end I began to lose faith in him again and I'm not really sure why. Maybe 60 per cent of me thought he was going to do the right thing. But somewhere in the back of my mind there was a voice saying he wouldn't. My confidence eroded at the time the intelligence officers were on. I call it the spook period. They didn't answer questions. There was so much blanked out. I suppose Saville had recourse to information that we didn't have, but that aspect of it disturbed me.

I thought it made a difference that he was flanked by judges from Australia and Canada. I know most family members felt they were still very much British establishment and there might be an element of that. But I'm a naturalised Canadian so, in some respects, I resented people casting aspersions on the independence of the Canadian judge, but that's quite a personal thing. Having lived in Canada for 30 years, I don't see them as being under British influence.

The Canadian judge, Hoyt, spoke very little so it was hard to assess him. Toohey, the Australian judge, was more actively involved. Nobody really knows when they went into their chambers how much they took in, or what their views were. One of the reasons I wanted to be there, particularly for the soldiers' evidence, was that a lot of times you try to judge body language. Listening to evidence is one thing, but to see how they reacted to a witness's remarks is something different and that was one of the things that I wanted to be there to see.

If I had to say yes or no as to whether I ended up trusting Saville, I'd have to say yes. But with a few niggling doubts.

PATSY McDAID

Saville was supposed to be independent but he favoured the soldiers. When they were under pressure, he told our solicitors they couldn't ask questions if another solicitor had already asked them, even if the questions hadn't been answered.

I don't think the other two judges make any difference. They were all picked by the British government and were all from areas that the British government controlled. It's not a matter of trusting them. It's just I know the truth, and the people of Derry know the truth and the only ones trying to hide the truth are the Brits. The reason I'm sceptical is that you could see the MoD crowd messing about and putting obstacles in the way all the time. From the start, I had no great faith in any of it. I'll wait 'til the end to see. We have the truth, but it's what Saville puts down that counts.

MICHAEL McKINNEY

I remember once, Glasgow was questioning a witness, who might have been involved with the IRA, regarding IRA men being interrogated, and Saville intervening and saying to Glasgow, 'How would you feel if you were hanging from a doorframe by the fingertips?' and I thought, 'This guy is in tune.' But there were other times. I think he protected Ted Heath.

Before the Inquiry, when we went to meet Mo [Mowlam] in London, we wanted an Irish judge, an international judge and a Brit, and we were told that we weren't going to get that, that we would get two Commonwealth judges. So it was the next best thing. And I have to say I was impressed by Toohey.

Hoyt seemed to ask questions which would've been in favour of the army's case. Toohey seemed to ask questions which would be seen to be in favour of the families' case. Maybe they balanced out.

CAROLINE O'DONNELL

I used to think if he has a heart he must know those soldiers are lying. But at the end of the day he is an English law lord.

I never really thought about the other judges much. I suppose they were appointed so the judges would not all be from England. They gave the impression that they didn't really want to be there. That's what I picked up from their body language. Lord Saville never gave that impression. I thought he was more human than the other two.

I know the time my father was up that Lord Saville apologised to him for being shot and told him that it should never have happened. That gave me a little bit of hope. The only other person that he actually apologised to was Bubbles Donaghey. I remember Bubbles coming down the stairs in the Guildhall crying after giving his evidence. It brought it all back. It's the English government that's responsible in the end, and we are just hoping they can come to terms with saying, 'We were wrong. We did murder those people. We are sorry.'

KATE AND PATRICK NASH

Kate: Somewhere along the line, I found a certain amount of respect for Saville. Not too much for the others because you never heard much from them, but for Saville himself. You had to be there watching his expression and you could see, especially when some of the soldiers were giving evidence, the man was cringing.

Patrick: It shows you the amount of things Saville was taking in that he was able to come in and ask questions himself. It was obvious he must have been doing a terrible amount of research because I never once heard him say anything that was irrelevant. Everything that came out was always pointed, he never called anybody a murderer but there are times you could actually feel he wanted to say that he saw through their lies.

Kate: You could more or less say the other two judges were British, being from Australia and Canada. If they'd wanted it truly international, they'd have had an American judge, possibly African, not even Irish because that might not have been fair. There were lots of other countries they could have chosen someone from. I don't think it was fair. I think the deck has been stacked against us. There was somebody in there with a big stick stirring because we never won any of those appeals about immunity or anything else. We won nothing. I think they would have preferred to have the Inquiry without us.

ALANA BURKE

Initially everyone was, 'Oh, he'll just be the same as before, he'll just be a British judge.' I changed my opinion about him a few times. From a personal point of view, the day that I gave evidence in the Guildhall I thought he was really kind, very human. When we were sitting in the gallery watching him, we used to think, 'He's not even listening, he's falling asleep', but he wasn't. Every little thing, he picked it up. He was so tuned in. But I think, if I was honest, he's still British establishment.

I think it was important there were three of them. If there was some point Saville didn't pick up, one of the other two would. The Canadian judge seemed to be very, very tuned in and interrupted proceedings quite a few times along the way, to get a point clear. If he didn't understand it, he would double-check and go back and re-question the legal representatives. From that point of view, it was a good idea that Saville had somebody either side of him.

JOHN KELLY

I think Saville was naive at the outset in that he thought he could do what he wanted. Whatever rulings he made, that was the law within the Inquiry. But his rulings were overturned, so he lost the power. There were other times when I thought he acted unfairly, for example when Edward Heath was giving evidence. It was the establishment protecting the establishment. Heath refused to answer about 50 questions. If a civilian had done that, he would have been charged with contempt, but Heath got away with it. That was fear within Saville, being a member of the establishment, a law lord, that he could be castigated for taking Heath on. Some of the civilian witnesses were treated badly by the army's lawyers and Saville allowed it to happen.

I found the Australian judge very interactive. He would ask more questions not only of the civilians but even of the barristers. I think this guy was trying his best. The other guy said very little, so that when he opened his mouth everybody sat up and gasped. He just sat there and listened and I found that strange. The positive thing was the very fact that we had three judges. If we go back to Widgery, there was only one and he could do what he liked. The two guys either side of Saville I think will have controlled him for the right reasons. I hope so anyway.

JOE MAHON

If you ask anybody to name the three judges, people only know Saville. They haven't a clue who the other two are. I don't know who they are. I couldn't tell you their names. Maybe they are genuine, just trying to do their job, but you can't do a job with your hands tied.

GERALDINE DOHERTY

The first time I saw Saville in the Guildhall chamber, I thought he was just ordinary, like ourselves. I did feel a bit iffy on him as well, but I thought, 'Well, maybe he'll give justice to the families, we'll just have to wait to see.' Sometimes since then, I've thought, 'Naw, he's not for the families.' Other times, I've thought that he is. He was very well mannered, I'll say that for him. And he's not slow. He was taking every tiny thing in.

At the start, when I thought of the three of them together, sometimes I was afraid we had no chance, on account of their backgrounds. I am still sceptical, especially because of the nail bombs being planted on Gerald. I ask myself, do they honestly think that somebody would be going about with four nail bombs protruding, and I feel, 'Aye, maybe they would.' At the end of the day, Saville is British.

There were definitely times Saville had one rule for them, another rule for our people. He protected witnesses for the government. He let lawyers for the Brits go in and out through our people. But he wouldn't let our solicitors question them like that. I was thinking, 'Hey, hold on there ....'

EILEEN GREEN

When they were questioning people you could be very impressed by how deep they would go. One thing I thought about Saville was how intelligent he was. Sharpest-minded person I ever watched. But, saying that, there was one day I walked out in protest. Some elderly man was giving his evidence, from Spain or somewhere, we didn't really know, on video. We didn't see him. It came about he had already been in England to give the statement he was being questioned about. So why couldn't he come back to give his evidence? They reckoned there were about six people in the room with him as he spoke, but we couldn't see them. We weren't even allowed to see him on the video screen. I couldn't listen to that. I said to my husband, 'I'm away, I'm not listening to this rubbish.' Of course, I was back in the next day.

JOHNNY CAMPBELL

It doesn't matter what Saville comes out with. There's a whole mass of stuff in the public domain now, all put on the table for anybody to go through and see. They'll see the truth. It's staring you in the face.

The man himself was OK. Of course, he was a British law lord, and you wouldn't know what was going on behind the scenes. So I wouldn't put my full trust on the line for him. Like everybody else, I thought there should have been an international figure as chairman, an American, for example. And there would have been a better spread if the other two judges hadn't come from Commonwealth countries.

I felt less trust when the decision was taken to hide the soldiers' identity, and then the decision to move to London. Admittedly, they were the result of Saville being overruled, but it's the same system. I thought they were going back to – Well, all right, you can have an Inquiry, but on our terms. Same with the weapons being lost from the MoD and the pictures going missing – You can have an Inquiry into all this, but ….

JIMMY DUDDY

We had had one head law lord in Widgery, who turned out to be a complete puppet of the establishment and betrayed all that should be held sacred in truth and justice. So when we got another British law lord, there was a very negative impression. We are all politically aware. We know of the other cases of killings involving the British establishment in the North, and the outcome has been to cover the backs of whoever was involved. A joke.

It would have been better to have an American civil rights judge or a South African, although at that stage you wouldn't have had many black judges in South Africa. There was always a doubt in the back of my mind.

Jimmy Duddy, now 52 (right), was a nephew of John Johnston (left, with his wife Margaret), married, a 59-year-old draper who was shot in the leg and shoulder when going to the aid of Damien 'Bubbles' Donaghey, and who died four months later. Jimmy Duddy is a painter and lives in Derry's Galliagh estate.

My father had great reservations. You only have to look at the Hutton Inquiry to see why. That was an open inquiry and it turned out a white-wash. It was blatantly scandalous. It really knocks you back. That makes you think, When push comes to shove, how will Saville be?

I started having my doubts watching Saville over in England during the evidence of the army. I thought he protected the soldiers, the MI5 people, the government people and the military police far too much. He stuck very rigidly to the rules of the Inquiry in terms of the questioning. He went into some areas that were getting good and then stopped. It was like opening the door into a room you really wanted to see into, having a wee look and then closing it. We wanted whatever was in there inves-tigated. But if our team came back and said, Let's just look in there again, Saville would stop it: Sorry, these questions have been asked .... But they weren't answered to our satisfaction.

This isn't a reflection on Christopher Clarke or his team, but they hadn't delved deep enough. Many's the debate our team had with Saville, want-ing an explanation why our questions were overruled.

When it came to repetitive questioning of IRA members, he didn't stop it. There would have been half an hour on the same question and never once did he say, 'That question has already been asked.' I started losing heart in Saville.

All the army people, everybody involved in that 18 months in England, had legal teams and they were all well drilled. Then when we came back to Derry, all the IRA had legal teams, and somebody would step in when it went too far overboard. But at times Glasgow in particular would have gone overboard tearing civilians apart, and Saville was the only protection they had. At times, he didn't give any protection.

It would be heart-breaking if it proved another sham. It's a lot of trust to have been put on one man's shoulders, especially a British law lord. At times from across the room, you could see he was exasperated by the lying. I watched his body language especially with Colonel Wilford. He never looked at him. If he asked him questions he looked away. You could see Saville's exasperation that this man, even after all of these years, who made a mistake which caused 27 people to be shot, still wouldn't admit doing anything wrong. Saville asked Wilford very hard questions. You could see he just didn't like the man and didn't like his attitude and lack of remorse.

BERNARD GILMOUR

Some days he was OK and other days he came out with things that made you think it was all going to go pear-shaped. Most of the time he was fair.

I think he treated the soldiers the exact same as he treated our witnesses. He wouldn't let the soldiers' lawyers harass our witnesses, and he wouldn't let our crowd harass the soldiers. It was pretty equal. A couple of times, he put his foot down. And having the other blokes on either side of him made a big difference. They are top men in their country. The first wee man went off sick and died. But the other two blokes picked up on everything, including things that maybe Saville didn't want to know. Like, if there was something that the soldiers didn't answer and Saville was for letting it go, one of the others would have jumped in and questioned him. Their presence was very important.

KEVIN McDAID

W hen Saville came over for the first time, it sounded great. But once the Inquiry started, it was different. I don't think civilian

Bernard Gilmour (next page) was one of eight children living in the Rossville Flats in the Bogside. He was seven years older than his brother Hugh (above), a tyre-fitter, who was 17 when shot dead from behind as he ran from the soldiers along Rossville Street. Bernard Gilmour is now a taxi driver, married, with four children, and lives in Creggan.

Bernard Gilmour

The Bloody Sunday Inquiry

witnesses from Derry were given fair treatment. When you look back at the soldiers, and even more so at Heath, questions were asked but there were no answers. We never got that degree of freedom. I think Saville could have been a bit more open. I remember during the summing up, Arthur Harvey asking a certain thing and Saville coming in and saying, 'Why didn't you ask that earlier on?' But he had asked it, and Saville had knocked him back. There were many questions we asked which were never answered.

People who went up to the witness stand did find Saville civil enough, but in general he didn't really help a lot. As it went along, he went down a mile in my regard. There was bias. The soldiers' solicitors seemed to get more of a free hand than ours did.

To me, whether it was Saville or any of the other two it was all the same. What I hope is that in the end they will have respect for the families and our legal teams, the same as the respect we showed them. But I am very, very wary, and so is the rest of my family. I'm withholding judgement.

MAURA YOUNG

For some, there is no trust there because he is English. Those other judges are British too. It's not an international inquiry, it's semi-British. We didn't really get what we should have but, like everything else, you have to pick up the ball and run with it. Mind you, Toohey was very good, he clarified questions, always asking for greater details.

LIAM WRAY

Saville is a clever man, nobody's fool and I reckon ten times smarter than Widgery. So I was ten times more worried. And as the Inquiry went ahead I realised that my fears were justified. He turned around in earlier days and made great rulings that the soldiers couldn't have anonymity and had to give evidence in Derry, and every time his rulings were overturned in the High Court. And people said,' Well, he did his best, but he had to accede to the other courts.' It's a great way to be. He's quite a character, doesn't miss a thing.

I liked old Somers, God have mercy on him, although he didn't say a lot. Maybe it was just because he stood outside the Guildhall and had a smoke and looked normal. I always got the feeling that Somers was a boy that wouldn't be anybody's man. Then they brought in Toohey and Hoyt. They were very hard to judge. I sat in that Guildhall just watching their expressions, listening to the witness but focusing on the judges, and they very seldom gave much away. For a while I thought Toohey was sleeping until he started to ask questions. Same with Hoyt. Then you realised they were wide awake. These are boys we are not used to. It's very difficult to know their mindset. What I do know is this: I don't trust them. I have seen how they gave more patience and tolerance towards the legal representation of soldiers than to the families. I am unhappy that I have been in a public inquiry where 47 per cent of the witnesses have been anonymous and five per cent have been screened, where there were Public Interest Immunity Certificates for countless documents. I don't trust Saville, I don't trust Hoyt and I don't trust Toohey.

I remember Muhammad Ali in an interview many years ago, somebody said to him, 'You don't like white people, some of your attitudes are hostile', and he said, 'No, I don't have a problem, I like white people.' Then he said, 'Well, let's put it this way. If somebody took you to a pit of snakes and said to you 80 per cent of them are all right, it's only the other 20 per cent that will bite you, you wouldn't jump in there, would you?' It's the same with this Inquiry.

MICKEY BRIDGE

Saville may have thought he was independent at the start. But when his opinions were referred back to him, I think he knew different. When it came to the question of the soldiers being at risk, there was no point of law. The High Court in London didn't tell him he was wrong on the law, but that he had made a wrong assessment. When he appealed that, Lord Woolf, who sat on the first hearing, also chaired the appeal – which I thought was horrendous. Woolf is now the Lord Chief Justice of England. I think Saville knew after that that if he did fight for his independence he would lose. The only place he had to go after the Appeal Court was the House of Lords, and if he had gone there and lost he would have had to stand down. So he gave up. You could see the result when the soldiers came to give evidence in London. Because they had anonymity, the pressure was off them. Remember it was the courts that gave the shooters anonymity, but it was Saville who extended it to the others. In doing that, he took potential witnesses away. He gave anonymity even to soldiers who said clearly they weren't asking for anonymity. One of them was a para. My conclusion is that Saville took the position that he was fighting the establishment, or sections of the establishment, and that he wasn't going to win, so he didn't fight on. Anybody listening to the evidence in London couldn't come to any conclusion except that at that point Saville was accommodating to the soldiers. That's not saying that Clarke didn't tackle the issues in a reasonable way. But take Soldier B, who shot either Bubbles Donaghey or Johnny Johnston, the man who caused the first casualty, and admitted that he went on to join the Special Air Service (SAS). He said he wasn't in the SAS on the day. Then he was allowed not to expand on that. It was an essential part of the day, those two men being tumbled down, the part that might have been the best help in explaining the whole day. I couldn't understand why Saville allowed Soldier B to be screened and allowed him not to explain what his role was on the day.

DAMIEN DONAGHEY

I t would have been better if it had been three international judges. Britain ruled the Commonwealth for long enough. Toohey seemed to be alert but when you looked at the other boy, you would have thought he was sleeping half the time. Saville is a smart man, no doubt about it. I think at the end up they were trying to make the IRA men fall guys. Martin McGuinness went in there for those couple of days. They were supposed to ask questions about Bloody Sunday. But Martin was hit with questions about months before Bloody Sunday and months after. If our barristers were to ask soldiers those kinds of questions, they were not allowed. So at the end I was a wee bit unsure. You couldn't trust Britain anytime, to be truthful.

I thought the buck should have stopped with Saville. If he turned around and said these questions cannot be asked, or that cannot be asked, that should have been it. But when the soldiers' lawyers lost it, they were allowed to take it to another court. The soldiers were caught out lying, every one of them, in London. There wasn't one of them who told the truth.

Heath was an ignorant cunt. He tried to take the families' barrister apart and call him this and call him that, and Saville stood and watched. The man had lost it, but he was able to do what he wanted. That's one of the things with Saville. He backed people like Heath up and never backed up the ordinary people who were telling the truth. There were civilian witnesses in Derry harassed when giving their evidence and Saville let it happen.

REGINA McKINNEY

I have a lot of confusion about Saville. At the beginning I would have been very open about him, believing that he'd be kind of looking at the whole picture, really seeing the truth as it was and not afraid to stand for it. As time went on, I wouldn't have had complete hope in him, because he seemed a wee bit prejudiced. He was kind enough, civil enough to the families, but we saw him correcting solicitors from one side and maybe not so much from the other. I'm really trusting in God when it comes down to it. I would have no trust in the Inquiry. But I believe God can move mountains and that's where my hope is.

3 Lawyers

MICKEY BRIDGE

There were some excellent lawyers and there was some I wouldn't let walk my fucking dog. There were some lawyers from the town that had agendas of their own which had nothing to do with Bloody Sunday. That surfaced over time. You got to know most of them fairly well. What they think of me is a matter for themselves. I don't give a fuck either, because they were there to give my point of view whether they represented me or not.

LIAM WRAY

I had great respect for my family's solicitor. Not very diplomatic, but very astute. For the duration, Greg McCartney was in contact with me every day, including weekends. What he didn't know he learned. He had a passion. It was more than just playing a legal role.

Legal people are a breed on their own. I was always impressed by Mansfield when he was strutting his stuff. He's a big name, has a big impact, and that's important, because when Michael Mansfield stands up to say something, the press listen and that is where half your battles are won, in public. Also, Saville would show Gifford and Mansfield a bit more reverence. They had worked in the same field and were familiar with that stuff.

For such a large team I was disappointed by Madden & Finucane. They really only had two people. Arthur Harvey, when he was good he was very good; when he was bad he was useless. Mind you, Arthur was on his feet most of the time, so it was easier for him to make a faux pas. The Madden & Finucane team were not pushing the political. From their opening statement, they were out to prove a cock-up, that it wasn't a thought-out thing, which negates the responsibility of the civil servants and the politicians. The implication was that individual soldiers had stepped out of line and some commanders didn't control their troops too well. That's nonsense, but it's where their team went to.

The chap from Madden & Finucane who questioned Heath was terrible, past his sell-by date. You have to be incisive in your questioning, and listen to the answers, and know when to move on. But Arthur was smart, had a nice demeanour, and was able to land a lot of good punches.

The dispute our family had about legal representation was a reminder that these people are paid professionals. When the tribunal is over, they get on to their next case. They won't carry any annoyance or frustration that we didn't get the truth or could have done better. To them, it is just a job.

But I think we broke the mould in a way that some of the lawyers were not happy with. Our family and others had no problem calling their barrister or QC and saying, 'I want a word with you', and saying, 'I think you should go this way or did you miss that?' Quite a few of them resented that. There is that class thing. Plus, if you look at normal court procedures, you don't talk to your barrister; you talk to your solicitor. But they were in the Inquiry in Derry, where they often had to deal directly with you. A lot of them found that extremely difficult, and didn't have the skills to do it.

With Michael Mansfield I had no problem, Tony Gifford, the same. Richard Harvey, the same. Kieran Mallon, no bother, Arthur Harvey. I think the reason some of them were uncomfortable dealing directly with a client was that the client would be emotional and passionate about the truth being exposed. They are colder fish. At the end of term, as I call it because they are like public schoolboys at times, the legal teams would get together for a drinking bash: the representatives of the soldiers and the representatives of the families. It was not personal to them. But to the families it was passionate. I couldn't have had a finer solicitor than Gregory McCartney. He understood what this meant to our family and the amount of our life it took up. So, as for the legal teams: like tradesmen, there's some of them good, and some of them not so good.

PATSY McDAID

O ur lawyers got up and questioned the soldiers and came out with some great points. Saville would get up and defend the soldier, taking the heat off him. The lawyers always seemed to rock them a bit by coming in and asking questions that were already asked. Then Saville would give the impression of defending the soldiers.

You expected nothing else from the soldiers' lawyers. They are there to do their job, back these boys up to the hilt. Half the time they weren't able. You could see them blatantly trying to get out of holes that they dug themselves into. It was the establishment looking after their own. Some of the lawyers were of the age that they wouldn't know what Bloody Sunday was. Sure they knew nothing about it.

CAROLINE O'DONNELL

I didn't like Glasgow. Even when you were walking along a corridor he wouldn't acknowledge you. I had the impression he thought we were all republicans, and the dirt of the day.

Obviously, I was more concerned with the Madden & Finucane solicitors who were representing our family. Brian McCartney was fantastic. Arthur Harvey was very good. Barry MacDonald, he was fantastic. And the man with the silver hair, Michael Mansfield. I thought his tactics were spot on. He brought one soldier to his knees. I think it might have been the McKinney family. I think it was the soldier who killed Mr McKinney. There are two McKinney families. It's the one with all the girls, the daughters. That day, there wasn't a dry eye in the place, everybody was just bawling and crying. That was the week of all the evidence from Glenfada Park. I mean there were four fellas all lying murdered beside each other, seven people shot in that small area within minutes. It must have been mayhem. Michael Mansfield's questioning brought all that back.

KATE AND PATRICK NASH

K*ate:* There were lawyers it would have been very hard to warm to. One exception would have been Lawson. He was the sort of man you could have had a bit of crack with.

P*atrick:* He was in there to fight a corner, and even the soldiers are entitled to a defence. But the way he did it was really aggressive. Glasgow, on the other hand had a different approach, very soft spoken. He was always apologising.

K*ate:* Always apologetic, but then like a shark. 'Please forgive me if I …' and, 'I'm not accusing you of …' and then he would strike. Christopher Clarke is a brilliant man. He would put you off with that plummy English accent but a brilliant man. I was very impressed with our family's lawyer, Mansfield, both as a lawyer and as a person. He's very, very smart. We learned a lot about him. Very genuine, very humane, very charming, fun to have around, a man who could leave his work at home. In fact, all our lawyers were good fun. It was a scream when we were socialising.

Patrick: We also liked Arthur Harvey. Very sharp. And Lavery, from Peter Madden's team. He questioned Edward Heath and I think they picked the right man to do the job. He showed Edward Heath up to be an idiot.

KAY DUDDY

I didn't like that they were representing soldiers and the government, but we actually got on quite well. In the end, we were quite friendly, which was something I never envisaged. What I found amazing was watching the different teams representing the families, representing the soldiers, representing former prime ministers, shaking hands and talking to each other. In my naivety, I didn't imagine that they could be friends with one another or that I could get on with them. Myself and the majority of the families, we felt it was important to let them see we were human

Former factory worker **Kay Duddy** (right) was the second eldest of 15 children living in the Creggan in January 1972. She was eight years older than Jackie, 17 (left), a textile worker, who was shot dead as he fled from the paras across the Rossville Flats car-park. He was the first person killed on Bloody Sunday. Kay Duddy now lives in the Moss Park area of Derry.

The Bloody Sunday Inquiry

beings like themselves, not their arch enemies. It was important that they saw us as people who had been wounded and lost loved ones, ordinary human beings. I imagined they had this thing that we were all hiding guns up our skirts. I think the vast majority of them went away thinking a little bit different about us.

It wasn't actually a court setting. People laughed at me because my two new words from the Inquiry were 'inquisitorial' and 'adversarial'. Prior to that, I couldn't pronounce them. But the fact that it was an inquisitorial inquiry kept a lot of the solicitors and barristers on a leash. They couldn't let rip the way they would normally have done because they had to keep it inquisitorial as opposed to adversarial. In an adversarial role, you would have seen the dog with the bone. At some stage, I would love to see them actually doing that.

JEAN HEGARTY

I don't have a huge opinion of the legal system so I'd have had no regard to lose as regards the lawyers' performance. I thought Michael Mansfield was very, very impressive and he's certainly effective. Most of the questioning was done by barristers but one of the most effective pieces of questioning was done by a solicitor, Barra McGrory. I thought his was the most effective questioning of the whole Inquiry. In terms of one person questioning another he really got to the point.

GERALDINE DOHERTY

I never liked the lawyers for the soldiers. When they were outside the chamber, they looked different. You might have passed them on the street, and said, 'Hello, how are you doing?', not thinking. But their body language was far from that in the chamber. Glasgow came across as very hoity-toity, trying to make our people look stupid and liars. I suppose it was just their job, representing paras. What else could they do? I used to notice them in the Guildhall looking over at where the families sat, checking to see how many were attending. That made it more important that we were always there, saying, 'Aye, here we are to fight you.'

As far as our lawyers were concerned, I only really took on Madden & Finucane. I thought Arthur Harvey came across really well, and especially Seamus Treacy, who was representing Gerald. You always think solicitors just do the job and have no feelings, but I will always remember Seamus Treacy standing up when they were opening the cases, saying that this was a young boy that was murdered, and I could hear it in his voice. His voice got weaker and shaky, as if he was nearly going to fall down into tears. He wasn't just a lawyer doing a job. I'll always remember that.

JOHN KELLY

I thought they were on a high pedestal, but when you sit down with them they are just human beings. There were some excellent times, when the families would love to have clapped. At other times, the head dropped. You would say to yourself, 'Jesus, what's that lawyer doing?' But at the same time, these were people who trained for this.

Through it all, the families still owned the process. We gave the process to the lawyers after the Inquiry was set up. I am not a lawyer, Mickey McKinney is not a lawyer, Gerry Duddy is not a lawyer. We couldn't have gone into the Inquiry and did the job they have done. But we could have sacked lawyers if we didn't like what they did. They were there to represent their clients, and if we weren't happy we could have sent them on their way. So the families still kept control.

JOHNNY CAMPBELL

It went on a very long time. There were days you were sitting there and they were talking for hours and you came out none the wiser. All that legal jargon and points of order. Unless you were educated in that language, you didn't have a clue.

Even so, I liked listening to the lawyers when they were on the ball. Mr Harvey impressed me, and Mansfield, because I thought that they were very direct. They were able to put the soldiers on the spot. From the families' point of view, I thought they were brilliant.

I got on with nearly everybody around the tribunal. The only people I disliked were the defence. Some of those boys, like Glasgow, were maybe only doing their jobs, but they seemed to be more concerned with what people were doing who had nothing to do with Bloody Sunday than with what actually happened on the day. They were on about the Provisionals and Officials. I thought they were going off track there, that they had another agenda. They didn't seem to be sticking to what the Inquiry was about. According to their questioning, it wasn't about what the paras had done, or the British government had done, even what Bogsiders had done, or the victims had done. It was about what people they wanted to highlight had done, even where they had no bearing on what happened at all.

MAURA YOUNG

I didn't like Glasgow. I found him very condescending. 'I am not calling you a liar but ....' Lawson was another upstart. He never even
introduced himself. Every lawyer gets up and introduces himself to the
witness but he never introduced himself. He had no manners. I liked
Christopher Clarke; there was something about him. Of course you have
Peter Madden and Lord Gifford and so on, on our side. I found Arthur
Harvey very good. Seamus Tracey was excellent and Barry McDonald. I
enjoyed him because himself and Saville would have had great banter
between them on points of law. At the end of the day, I suppose they
were all doing their jobs.

TERESA McGOWAN

I thought Arthur Harvey was great. He would speak to you personally.
One time, I explained to him something that was worrying me. You felt
comfort in the families and in the fact that the solicitors could come and
talk to you and be at ease with you.

The soldiers' lawyers were hostile when they were questioning our
witnesses. That was their job. They had to go on that way. But they would
have said good day when they passed you in the Guildhall. I think there
were quite a few of them good solicitors.

Teresa McGowan, 62 (left), is the widow of
Daniel McGowan (right), who was shot and
wounded as he sought cover at Joseph
Place. A mother of six, Teresa McGowan lives
in the Lone Moor Road area of Derry.

ALANA BURKE

There was one barrister representing the soldiers and the very look of him terrified me, just something about him. I kept thinking before going up to give evidence, 'If he gets up to question me, I'll fall apart.' He just had this awful demeanour. And he did get up to question me. I thought to myself, 'Just keep going, keep going, keep going, he's trying to bring you down.' I thought to myself, 'Right', and I remember thinking, 'I'll stare at him.' I tried to tune into what way he was thinking. But in the end up, I did break down, and I hated myself for it. It was painful.

Arthur Harvey impressed me very much. And I suppose Glasgow was very good at his job. As a lawyer, he was very good.

KEVIN McDAID

The soldiers' lawyers twisted things on behalf of their clients. Most of the people that gave evidence in Derry had been there on the day. They were cross-questioned and they took it on the chin. But our solicitors couldn't question the soldiers in the same way. Saville stopped them.

JIMMY DUDDY

I would say Arthur Harvey, Barry McDonald and, obviously, Mansfield and Gifford were tops. And even if you don't like it you have to have respect for Glasgow and them who were doing a great job for the soldiers and MoD. They were good. At times I would feel contempt for them, but that was because they were doing their job so well.

JOE MAHON

One boy came up and asked me more or less was I telling the truth, and I said, 'Are you calling me a liar?' He kept changing the wording about and I said, 'Are you still calling me a liar?' I don't know how I kept my composure. I was looking to go down and hit him, the anger was that bad inside me. All I said to the Inquiry was what I saw. At that point, Saville said to him, 'Mr Mahon is answering your question', and that was it. But what I saw it as was, 'Croppy, lie down.' They give you an Inquiry and then they keep you quiet.

They showed me pictures of the para and I picked him out in the video, then they showed me a picture of him in civvies and I picked him out in civvies. One of the bullets that came from his rifle was found inside Gerald

Donaghey. He was shot in Abbey Park, yet that soldier said he wasn't near Abbey Park. He'd had to pass Jim Wray to get to shoot Gerald Donaghey. That did come out in cross-examination. The lawyers were doing their best, I suppose.

REGINA McKINNEY

I wasn't impressed by the Crown lawyers. If they were really looking to find the truth they would have told their clients to tell the truth. I mean, they had immunity for anything they'd say from the witness stand. It wasn't going to lead to them being imprisoned. As far as I'm concerned, the only people who wasted public money were those who went to the Inquiry knowing they weren't going to tell the truth, or who kept saying, 'I don't remember.' I can't understand how a soldier who was 19 or 20 at the time can turn around and say he doesn't remember killing people, doesn't remember them lying dead beside him. I was eight and I can remember.

The soldiers' lawyers' line of questioning was all the same. It wasn't about finding out the truth. And then our lawyers couldn't go back over the same questions.

MICHAEL McKINNEY

Arthur Harvey, Barry McDonald, all of the Madden & Finucane team, they were all very good. Michael Mansfield was brilliant. I thought Lawson, for the army, was a great lawyer. If I got into bother and had to have someone represent me, I'd pick Lawson. I think Glasgow was patronising. A good lawyer, but very patronising.

BERNARD GILMOUR

Your man Glasgow. Smart boy.

4 Media

JIMMY DUDDY

They were there and then they would have forgotten about us. Obviously the local papers carried it every day. But the English press weren't interested, bar when one of the big witnesses came along, or when it turned into, 'Let us discover the complete ins and outs of the IRA in 1970 and 1971.'

They shoved in this name Infliction, the so-called agent who may or may not exist who stated that years after Bloody Sunday he heard Martin McGuinness saying that it was him that fired the first shot. This was complete nonsense, but it didn't matter. It took six or seven months to prove it was complete nonsense. One of the tactics that Allan Green had when soldiers or any of MI5 or the RUC Special Branch were on was to get up at the end and ask this one question, 'Do you know any evidence that has come to your knowledge over the years that Martin McGuinness fired the first shot?' 'Martin McGuinness accused at Bloody Sunday Inquiry' was what would have been reported in the news. The soldier or intelligence officer might have been torn to ribbons, or might have just said no, but the question served the purpose.

I'll give you an example of Captain Condor. He was the intelligence officer of one of the battalions in Derry and his most important evidence was about the car that was bringing Gerry Donaghey to the hospital. His evidence was that a car turned around the corner of the bridge and the driver got out and ran away. He told the rest of the soldiers to stand back and he went up, saw the body, saw the nail bombs. His evidence was lies because the evidence of one the other soldiers was that it was him who had actually driven the car from Barrack Street to the bridge and that nobody got out and ran away. This should have been massive news. Gerry Donaghey was the only person shot on Bloody Sunday that the Brits were saying had guns or nail bombs on the body. And, remember, that's what Widgery found. Here was that evidence being contradicted by a soldier.

Everybody listening knew it was a big development. Captain Condor was asked by our team very directly, 'Did you plant the nail bombs? Did you know the police officers who planted the nail bombs?' Obviously, he said no. It should have been 'Officer denies planting bombs', or 'Officer is accused of planting bombs', something like that. Green got up and asked his usual questions, 'Had any intelligence come to you over the years that Martin McGuinness fired the first shot?' That is what was reported from that day in the papers.

KATE AND PATRICK NASH

Kate: There was a cartoon in one of the papers about me when we were in London that was an absolute lie. It showed me chewing gum. I don't chew gum. And Linda objected to the fact that because of the way we were sitting they had her as the fat one and me as the slim one and she is the one who was slimming. You could laugh that off, but it was very petty of the reporter. And then he said we were flying in and out at will. It was never like that.

The media weren't there for the time the television screen got anonymity. Now that was a thing. A TV screen being screened. There was this guy from the intelligence services in France or wherever giving evidence with one of the MoD solicitors sitting beside him telling him what to say. They hid the video screen in case anybody saw him. An anonymous man speaking from nobody knows where with the video screen screened. All you could do was laugh. You'd think at least one of the papers would have put that in. But no.

Patrick: They weren't there either when this soldier who was only 18 on Bloody Sunday said he fired his rifle only when he was asked to. They asked him had he ever fired his rifle since, and he said yes. Then he was asked, 'Did you kill anybody?' and he replied, 'Lots of people.' You'd think that was news. But the newspapers didn't refer to that, either.

Kate: I think the government manipulates a great deal of people through the newspapers, and Saville is probably manipulated too. He may not see it as that, he might just see it and say, 'Well, this is the way things are done.'

Patrick: The media talked about the cost of this Inquiry and compared it to the Hutton Inquiry, which paled into insignificance. Now, I didn't get involved too much in the cost argument. I can't break down all the costs. But I do know that every time the army or MoD went for judicial review, it was costing them thousands upon thousands. We never took them once to judicial review. We accepted what was thrown at us, we fought the corner, but we lost them all. And about flying in and flying out at will. We didn't want to go to London. We would have rather stayed in Derry. We had to go to London. We didn't ask for the Dolphin Square Hotel. If they had put us into a hostel, we would have said, 'Well, this is the way it's done. We aren't used to it anyway.' So I don't know what they can put down to us in terms of the expense. But in some of the papers, it was all put down to us.

MICHAEL McKINNEY

John and myself would have been close to the media and they would have been close to us. I would've liked more play from the media. It wasn't to be, probably for a number of reasons. They have to report on the evidence and give it as they hear it, but I think there were times when that actually just didn't happen. I think they were very selective at times. Certainly, I would have expected more coverage when the soldiers were giving their evidence.

I was livid at the close of the oral evidence, when I read a statement on behalf of the families on the Guildhall steps. All the families were around me. Then Gregory Campbell appears on the scene, complaining about the cost. They didn't interview one of the families or ask us how we felt now that 900-odd witnesses had given their stories of Bloody Sunday. The topic on news reports that night was Gregory Campbell complaining about the costs again. Things like that really pissed me off. A lot of the reporters were rowing their own boats. As long as they got a story, it didn't matter what it was. I was very, very disappointed, especially with the local media. I don't think that the statement I read out that day was carried anywhere.

Looking back, I think we should have been tighter, kept more control. There were times we should have said to reporters, 'No, we have nothing to give you on this.' We should have kept our powder dry. Some of the stories that came out had no strong, detailed information. We were always being asked to comment on the latest from Gregory. The old tune about costs was all he had. It was played out. Us making a comment only helped make it into a story.

KAY DUDDY

We had great local support. But the English papers basically didn't want to know, the *Daily Mail* being one of them. They sent out their spies in London and the worst they could come up with was that a few were chewing gum in unison. What sort of news is that? They tried stitching one of the legal team, too. I think the headline was 'Smarmy Marmy', about Michael Mansfield.

JOHNNY CAMPBELL

There's a man in this town called Gregory who whether he likes it or not is the same as me, a Derry Campbell. All he's done is go on and on about the costs of it all. But if my father hadn't been affected, if people hadn't been shot down, there would have been no costs. Every time Gregory spoke, it was all over the media. If the Inquiry had been done right the first time, there'd have been no costs. The media didn't once point that out to him. It's the powers that be who are to blame for the costs. Gregory's argument wasn't with us, but he made it with us, and the media went with him.

MICKEY BRIDGE

There were times when the media had things before my lawyers had them and they came directly from the Inquiry. That was wrong, the fault of the staff of the Inquiry. Even now, things are appearing in the papers that I never had any awareness of.

The media tended to appear when personalities appeared. On day-to-day reporting, things happened in the Inquiry that were never reported. Either the media just wasn't there or they didn't want to cause controversy. The reporting over in England was nonexistent except when some major politician appeared.

The British newspapers are what they are. They are controlled by the institutions, the sections of the government that we are attacking. So attacks were to be expected back. That's all there is to it.

KEVIN McDAID

In general, we stayed away from the media. You'd see certain people and the media were all over them, whereas the families and individuals who should have got a bit more coverage were hardly noticed. The media go for the big point not the genuine point.

They didn't come to us at any stage and ask if we wanted to add anything. I mean, when you are up in the witness box, they are only asking you what they want to ask you, and you can't say what you want to say. So there's things that you believe should have been said, but you weren't asked them. Nobody in the media ever followed that up.

EILEEN GREEN

I thought the English media were disgraceful. The only TV channel to pick it up was Sky News. When we went back to the hotel at night we always put Sky News on. And that's even though this was a very historical event. Even the place it was held in was very historic. Gandhi gave his first speech in England there. The first United Nations meeting was held there. And then us. But for some reason they played it down. When did a prime minister or ex-prime minister ever have to get up and answer to people like us before? But there was very little publicity about it.

BERNARD GILMOUR

Whenever Paisley appeared, the world's media was there. But they never appeared for when the soldiers that killed my young brother were there. When Martin McGuinness was on they went mad. But when I was on, or anybody else whose brother or father was killed, they didn't bother. No cameras, no media, no nothing. I never bothered about them. I gave my evidence and then a fella came up and said, 'Do you want to give a statement for the paper?' I said, 'No, you can get my statement off the tribunal.' I knew they weren't going to ask me how my mother was after my brother died, how my father was. They just wanted to know was there an IRA man there. They were just witch-hunting for the IRA. So I just said I wasn't talking to the media at all.

PATSY McDAID

I wouldn't give a damn what the English papers say. I never read them. I wouldn't buy them. Anybody who attended the Inquiry would have had to be very dumb if they didn't see what was going on. These boys were lying their heads off. If Saville had been sitting there in a court and listening to all that evidence, he would have turned around and said, 'Look, boys, I don't have to go any further, you are guilty and that's it.' That's what a jury would have said, instead of waiting years to go through all this. But you wouldn't get that from the media. The English papers tried to play it up throughout the world that we are terrorists, bombers. You would have had to be a blind newspaper man not to see the truth, not to see that Widgery was a farce. But they insisted on highlighting a riot if a march took place. They would take away from the march by highlighting the rioting. So the idea would be, these people are just rioters. So that when it came to Bloody Sunday, people would think it was rioters who were shot. I wouldn't buy an English paper even today, looking at the stupid things they come out with.

There are wains starving in this world and all that is happening in Iraq and they'll come out with [David] Beckham going with another woman, or so and so is doing such and such. The only time they highlight a story is when it suits them and it suits their needs. That's how it has been with Bloody Sunday over the years. There was rioting, yes, but only because there were cops there and Brits there. We weren't allowed to march and then they showed their presence with force and it was only natural that the young boys would fight back in anger. The papers didn't say, 'What is the need for these boys to be here, these cops or Brits, provoking the situation?'

I think over in England a lot of people wouldn't know what the Saville Inquiry is. When you are in a taxi over there and they say, 'Oh you're from Ireland', and you would say, 'We are over for the Saville Inquiry', and they would say, 'What's that?' One taxi driver did have an idea about it, but nobody else had the foggiest. That's because over there it was never highlighted. What they got over there was, 'These are terrorists, and it all happened 30 years ago anyway.'

JEAN HEGARTY

I know a number of people were very disappointed in the media coverage while we were in London. Basically, we didn't have any. Then when Heath was on there was a certain amount of coverage. That annoyed me. But I really had no expectations of media performance. I know a lot of people were sick of hearing about Bloody Sunday. What there was was just about selling newspapers.

DAMIEN DONAGHEY

The media was a joke. When the Inquiry started they were there for a couple of days, then they disappeared. But the minute Martin McGuinness turned up to give evidence, there was press everywhere. Myself and Gerry Duddy came out with a banner saying, 'It is a Bloody Sunday Inquiry, not an inquiry on Martin McGuinness.'

Where were they when the main soldiers who killed people were giving evidence in London? Not to be seen. The only press I talked to in

London was on the day the soldier who shot me was giving evidence. I think it was BBC Radio 2.

Mrs McGuigan went over to London and was in tears when they showed photos of her husband lying in the morgue. She had to be helped out. I know London is a big place and Bloody Sunday wouldn't be a major thing to them. But you'd think they might mention that scene with Mrs McGuigan. But not at all. Then, the minute Martin McGuinness was up, there wasn't a newspaper in the world that wasn't interested. I think that's totally wrong.

LIAM WRAY

You could get angry with the media every day of the week. None of them did anything too bad. Some of the journalists were clearly reading the statements that had been supplied to them in advance but not hearing the evidence that came out in the box during questioning on the statements. There was a bit of frustration at that until we wised up. The journalists were very dispassionate, so for people involved watching the Inquiry every day, they had missed the passion that was there, and missed out what it was really about. But that was newspeople just doing their job. In general terms, they were fair. An odd time, it was not accurate. But, sure, there'll be a fish supper wrapped in it tomorrow.

Some particular papers did seriously annoy people. But what do you expect from a pig other than a squeak? You expect that from the British press. It wouldn't matter if it was the Falklands or the Gulf, they have to play the game the way they play the game. That's how they sell newspapers. Some tried to be more anti-Irish than the others to suit their audience. I wouldn't worry about it.

GERALDINE DOHERTY

I never took the media on. I think the other family members who spoke to the media put it across very well. But the British media would twist things, and only put the Inquiry in when it was going for them, when there was a bit of good evidence for their side. They would do a write-up on that. But you can be sure there'd be no write-up for evidence that was on our side.

ALANA BURKE

The media? They were always there in numbers when there was somebody like Father Daly giving evidence, or John Hume or Martin McGuinness. I didn't really have any contact with them. The only thing that affected me was a couple of times coming out in the evening when the Inquiry was over, and, according to what had been on, all these cameras. I'd wait 'til everybody went or else try and slip past. I hated all those cameras in your face.

JOHN KELLY

The local media were dead on, but the main media showed little interest. I expected that, because I'd looked at the Lawrence inquiry. You might get them in for the first day but the second day they were gone. Some people felt that when we went to London they'd be there in strength every day, but it didn't happen. It seemed to be certain times and individuals they were interested in. The British more or less ignored it because, basically, they didn't want to inform their public of what their soldiers did in Derry on Bloody Sunday.

MAURA YOUNG

All these common people took the stand and there was no media there. But the big high-profile witnesses, who weren't even there on the day, got great attention. The normal people were just ignored. Martin McGuinness … you would have thought it was his inquiry, the

amount of people in the media seats that day. That's just an observation. Personally, I had no bother with the media. When they were there, there they were, and when they weren't, there they weren't.

Maura Young, a former factory worker, was one of a family of eight from Westway in the Creggan. She was six years older than John (centre in photo on page 75), a shop worker, 17 when he was shot and killed at the Rossville Street barricade. Divorced, with two children and two grandchildren, Maura Young now lives in Shantallow in Derry.

5 Heath

JOHNNY CAMPBELL

One good thing was that it dragged in Edward Heath. That was rubbing their nose in it. That was satisfying. I was happy about that. And the higher echelons of the British Army having to sit and be cross-examined, I enjoyed that too. It didn't matter what they said. It was the fact that they were being put through the mill. That sort of thing had been unheard of before, but here it was. I enjoyed sitting and listening to our barristers giving them a grilling. They were lying, but it didn't matter.

They all lied. Heath is just a liar, full stop. The fact that he had to lie shows that Bloody Sunday went to the top. He knew it and the rest of them knew it and they had to try to lie their way out of it. It was the soldier done it on the street, but he was only the tool, the man carrying out the order.

JEAN HEGARTY

There was a lot of media hype about Edward Heath taking the stand but basically he said nothing. I think politicians are one of the lowest forms of life on this planet. And that goes for any politician really, so I had no expectations of them. I don't think they would know the truth if it stood up and bit them. They all have a way of not answering questions.

There were few answers from the spooks, either. Even now, you really have no idea what part they played, what kind of intelligence they fed in. You see all these events in Iraq now, how they had all this information about weapons of mass destruction, and you just think, 'How could they have had it so wrong?' I think that the spooks have significant questions to deal with about Bloody Sunday, none of which has been answered at the Inquiry. That's a failing of the Inquiry, that there was so much information we didn't have access to, that was redacted. The judges may have had access to a lot more information than we did, but I don't think that the intelligence agents answered any questions.

It makes you wonder, as far as the politicians are concerned, how much do their underlings tell them? I keep thinking back to that programme *Yes, Minister*. He would say one thing and they would go and do something and they would tell him they did it but they wouldn't tell him the nitty gritty of it. You just wonder how much that reflects real life.

MICKEY BRIDGE

S aville bent over backwards to accommodate Heath. Any time he got in difficulty there was a break. Heath went out and had a consultation with somebody and came back and formulated an answer. That happened on a regular basis. The same happened with Carrington.

They didn't give explanations or justifications. Even in relation to the briefing Heath gave Widgery about the stance he should adopt in chairing the first Inquiry, reminding him it was not just a military war but a propaganda war, he explained that as a general conversation about the situation in Northern Ireland. This was a British prime minister giving instructions to a man conducting a tribunal of inquiry and he was allowed to get away with it! There were different standards adopted towards witnesses. An example was when Bishop Daly gave evidence. He was sick at the time. But when it was suggested to Lord Saville that he leave through the side door to avoid the reporters he was told this couldn't happen. But it happened in England with Heath and Lord Carrington. They were escorted out a back door. Nobody was allowed anywhere near. Different standards for different witnesses, from Derry to London.

ALANA BURKE

E dward Heath was just not taking any responsibility whatsoever. Same old story. But most of the families think the orders came from the highest office in the land, and that was Edward Heath. As regards getting a prime minister on a stand to give evidence, that was something that you never thought would happen. Never. That was an achievement. He seems to have felt intimidated by the whole thing. 'How dare they? I'm an old man, Blah, blah.' But, at the end of the day, he has to take responsibility. He was the head of the government.

TERESA McGOWAN

I was amazed Heath got away with the stuff. I remember this girl went up, a journalist, she didn't want to give names of the people who spoke to her, and I think they were going to charge her. I thought that was awful when I saw the way that Heath went on. Sometimes I think they are waiting until he dies before telling the truth about Bloody Sunday. It might come out when he is dead. He just washed his hands of things, didn't speak, didn't answer, brushed it all under the carpet. That was the difference between him and somebody trying to do good.

MAURA YOUNG

Heath was all, 'How dare you ask me questions like that?' I didn't like him. But they tried to make him the fall guy: 'You gave the order, we were only following.' In fact, they weren't following anybody's order. It was just, get in there and teach those people a lesson. That made me angry too, talking to us as if we were stupid. We are all intelligent people. They think the Irish know nothing. I could nearly be a lawyer myself at this stage.

PATSY McDAID

I never really listened to Heath's evidence because I wasn't there. I did get the transcripts of his evidence and his statements but I'm not really into reading stuff like that because I know it's all rubbish. That's the difference between the two of us. We have nothing to hide, they have everything to hide. Heath is trying to protect himself, the general is trying to protect himself, the other boys all down the line, they're trying to protect themselves, and all of them are lying their heads off. I wouldn't be bothered with their evidence.

KATE NASH

Lavery showed Edward Heath up to be an idiot. His head wouldn't take in that he'd actually been brought there to give evidence. 'How dare you do this to me?' How dare anybody bring him there to answer questions! But when you do wrong you have to answer to somebody, even if you are Edward Heath. I couldn't believe that somebody that stupid could run a country, which is why I think there has to be other people behind the scenes running countries.

LIAM WRAY

Sometimes I now think that civil servants are more the government than politicians, because politicians come and go but the civil servants carry

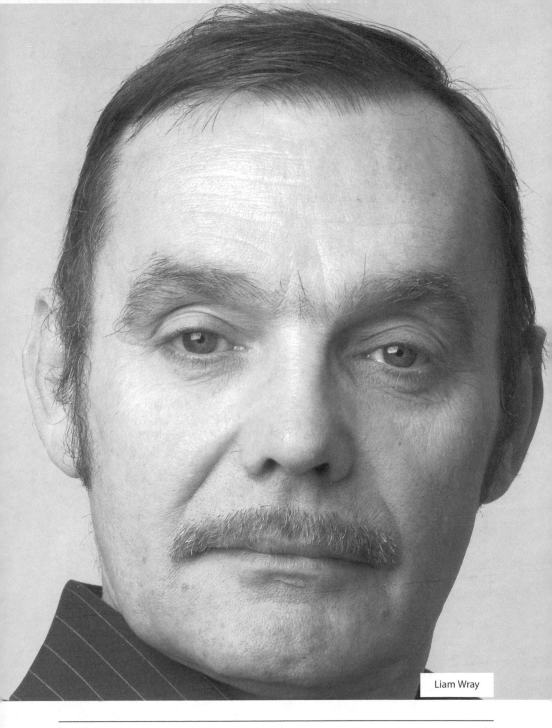

Liam Wray

Liam Wray (photo previous page), an electrician, was 18 on Bloody Sunday, from a Bogside family of nine. His brother, Jim (extreme right in the photo above) was four years older. Jim was shot as he fled from the soldiers across Glenfada Park, then shot again in the back and killed as he lay wounded on the ground. Married, with four children and four step-children, Liam Wray now lives in Foyle Springs in Derry.

the thread through. The feeling you get from them is that there's one benchmark, and all the rest have to accommodate to the British way or the British interest. You get that feeling. But they are people who are very hard to pinpoint in terms of responsibility.

Even though I attended every day for six years, there were times I lost my way, and didn't understand how government worked, how different departments overlap. You could see when non-advice was as pertinent as the advice that was being given.

We did get the minutes of a lot of meetings. Now they are just minutes. A lot of things are said that the civil servant does not write down, which he knows not to write down. So much of the evidence you need is not in the minutes. And any minutes that are missing are the ones with stuff that they hadn't time to sanitise. You sit and think people in ministerial positions would not talk about murder or shooting people, but I have no doubt they do. I have no doubt that coarse and base language is used that you never see. The civil servant is the astute boy, the civil servant can say a sentence that can mean a thousand things but those at the meeting understand. For public consumption, it is all different.

I think all those boys have influence. The ministers listen to them, the prime minister depends on them, they are the pulse of what is going on, going into different meetings, getting different views and carrying it back. It is an eye-opener for ordinary people to see how the system works. Most of what they say is low key, measured and often not very fruitful.

CAROLINE O'DONNELL

A lot of the evidence of civil servants and intelligence agents was lies, lies, lies, even more so than politicians, which didn't surprise me. I thought: what's the point in them even being called. Their main response was, 'I don't recall.' They could recall stuff when it was the soldiers' barristers who were cross-examining them. They had selective memory loss when it was our barristers. I would say they were well primed before they went in and told how to get out of a situation. It was very hard to sit and listen.

KAY DUDDY

To think that you had Ted Heath sitting there saying, 'At the end of the day, on the day these deaths happened, all I was interested in was getting my boat ready to go out sailing.' Only the fact that they were in there, that they were part of the Inquiry, that they had to put themselves out to appear, only that gives a little bit of hope.

JOHN KELLY

Heath was an arrogant person. I watched how he dealt with his cross-examination. Fifty times he refused to answer questions. I found that very hard to take – an ex-prime minister giving the excuse that he was dealing with the crew of his yacht when word came in. That's rubbish. He knew what was happening. What we had was contempt for the Inquiry. Carrington was the same. Michael Lavery who cross-examined Heath on our behalf was brilliant, tore him to shreds, but he still wouldn't answer questions.

As for Unionist politicians, they don't see the big picture. They can't see Bloody Sunday as a human rights issue. They look at it only as a republican issue. So, they see it as a waste of money. But you can't put a price on life or truth. My brother's right to life was taken from him. I find it offensive for people to slag off the Inquiry because of money and the time that it's taken. The only price put on my brother's life was £250 given to my mother. So that's what his life was worth to the British government then. They say this Inquiry has cost over £150 million. I don't give a shit if it costs £500 million.

MICHAEL McKINNEY

Sure, Heath didn't have any evidence. He refused to answer questions. He was disrespectful to our lawyer. The man was pathetic. He was a liar, too.

EILEEN GREEN

Heath didn't come across to me as a very intelligent man, although, in fairness, he was a good age.

6 Soldiers

MAURA YOUNG

I was expecting some of them, especially the shooters, after 35 years, to tell the truth. They were not going to get prosecuted as a result of their evidence. Even Saville said to a couple of them, 'This is your chance now, after all this time, to tell as much as you know.' A few days I was quite angry, especially when they were talking about the three at the barricade, which is where John was. You wouldn't have done it to a dog in the street. There was one boy came on and he was one of the boys that picked up a body at the barricade and he said he will never forget the young boy's face, and I was squealing inside me, 'Show him a photograph, show him a photograph, let it haunt him for the rest of his life.'

MICHAEL McKINNEY

Soldiers were given immunity from prosecution to come in and tell the truth and they came in and lied their heads off.

The Parachute Regiment proved themselves to be a closed unit. None of them gave detrimental evidence against the other. Not one. None of them said that he seen any particular soldier shooting an unarmed person. In the early stages of the Inquiry, the Brits' lawyers were maintaining that more than 30 bodies of gunmen had been carried over the border into the Donegal hills and buried, so as to hide IRA casualties. Any time a witness picked a place for a body and then somebody else put the body a few yards away, Glasgow and the others said, 'Ha, that's two bodies, and the one of them unaccounted for must be an IRA man.'

Soldiers A and B came in regarding the shooting of Damien Donaghey and John Johnston. Damien Donaghey was branded as a nail bomber back in 1972. But here we had A and B saying that they both shot a nail bomber but that it wasn't Damien Donaghey or John Johnston, because the Brits had already accepted that the dead and wounded had all been innocent.

Michael McKinney (left), from a family of 10 living in the Creggan, was 20 on Bloody Sunday, seven years younger than William (right), a compositor with the *Derry Journal,* who was shot dead as he stood with his hands up in Glenfada Park. Now a taxi-driver, Michael McKinney lives with his wife and three children in the Carnhill estate.

And that was the stage set, as far as the 'missing casualties' were concerned. Even with regard to the shooting of Jackie Duddy, they maintained they were shooting at somebody else who was armed. In all those cases, no evidence was given against any of the soldiers by any of their comrades. That's the game they played. It made me very, very angry.

But there were two soldiers that I do admire – the two who were in the car with Gerald Donaghey. One of them admitted putting the barrel of his rifle under a prisoner's chin. My reading of him and the other one was that they were telling the truth. Detrimental evidence had been given against one of them for something that he had done and he admitted that. Then they both went on and said they saw no nail bombs on Gerald Donaghey. Those two soldiers did impress me.

I was always hoping that there might be a couple who would come and give evidence against the shooters. But there was only 027, plus one or two outside the Paras. One of those gave evidence about the shooting of Hugh Gilmore. He was stationed on a roof at the end of Sackville Street overlooking the whole scene. He said he'd seen this soldier at the end of Block One shooting after this person running away, and Saville questioned him a number of times to the effect of, 'Are you telling me that you seen this soldier shooting at someone who was running away?' and he said yes. I think he questioned him about two or three times, from different angles, to get different answers from him but he got the same answer all the time.

He had seen a para shooting a man running away. But nothing came out from within the paras themselves.

All down the years, I listened to Derek Wilford blaming politicians. But in the witness chair, he never once blamed politicians. He never once pointed upwards. He didn't blame anybody. After Wilford finished giving his evidence, I thought, 'This is going to end up on the head of the foot soldiers.' Wilford had been hung out to dry for Bloody Sunday by the politicians. They put it all down to bad soldiering on the day. Nothing to do with them. If I had been Derek Wilford I would have been looking for my couple of days in that chair.

He held back. He was the only guy from the Paras who down the years I remember coming on TV and giving interviews about what happened. But when he sat in that chair he was a different person.

Those paras knew what they were doing. They enjoyed it. There was other evidence that Saville wouldn't look at regarding things that they'd done in Belfast before they ever came to Derry. It wasn't them all. Thank God it wasn't them all. If it had been all of them there would have been a couple hundred dead. I would put it down to about nine soldiers who possibly all worked together and knew that they were going in to do the business. Then the rest of the paras stood by them.

KEVIN McDAID

I was nervous about giving evidence, so I talked to Peter Madden and he said, 'Just tell the truth.' That's what the advice was from my solicitor. I don't know what was the advice the soldiers' solicitors gave them. Certainly, they were briefed. I mean, for them to say what they said, they had to have been told what to say. But they didn't seem to have been told to tell the truth.

GERALDINE DOHERTY

Over in London for the week that they were dealing with my uncle's case, I thought, we won't find any hope here, because of what I knew about the way they left him in the car to die. Then I saw the soldier for the first time who had driven him to the barracks. He was sandy-haired, very skinny, and came across as if he had a barrier around him protecting himself. When he started to speak, I still thought, 'Naw, there's no hope here.' But I came away happy, because he said that when he looked into the car there had been no nail bombs. He even said, 'Look, I wouldn't have got into that car if there had been nail bombs in it, I wouldn't have driven that car at all.' I thought, 'Well, there's one who is telling the truth at least.' After I listened to that soldier, I walked away with a song in my mind.

I remember one other soldier on the stand who was totally ignorant. At one time he pointed over to us in the family seats like we were murderers and terrorists, and he was cursing about us. I thought, he shouldn't be allowed to do that. Saville should have struck him down straight away. They were getting nowhere with him but they let him go on and on. If it had been one of us on the stand we would have been shot down on the spot.

PATSY McDAID

Your man Jackson is in charge of the whole British Army and he couldn't remember what happened on Bloody Sunday. He couldn't remember the truth. Typical.

It got to you when you had to listen to it. Even when it was shown on video, the boy sitting there would deny it. This one boy in particular, when they showed him the video of them actually coming into the Bog, up to Glenfada Park, he said that he wasn't moving his men forward until these armoured cars had come up to protect them from being shot at. But the film showed all his men at the wall at the archway, and there's not one armoured car in the place.

The next thing, he says only six of his men went into Glenfada Park, but the video shows them all climbing over the wall – 17 of them. They said to him, 'Where did the other eleven or twelve disappear to?' And he still said he waited for armoured cars to come up and only six of his men went into Glenfada Park. He stuck by it. Anybody else would have said, 'I'd better get out of this', but he still maintained that what he said was right. That's what you're up against. They just denied the truth even when it was there in front of them for everybody in the Tribunal to see.

Another boy, a top officer, was shown coming in, in a wagon with a plastic top where he could see everything, but he saw nothing. Even when he got out of his vehicle and the boys around him were shooting, he couldn't see them shooting. The Inquiry lawyer was saying, 'That's you there on the film, that's you driving in with the transparent shield', and he still said 'No, nothing happened like that.' That's what would drive you mad.

There were boys you could see their faces and boys behind screens, officers or privates, a sergeant or a so-called intelligence officer, they all came out the same. They must have been briefed to say, 'I can't remember.' Our solicitors couldn't turn around and say, 'You said this or you said that', if they said nothing. A couple of soldiers drifted away from just saying, 'I can't remember', and our solicitors were on top of them and had them muddled up. That's when Saville would try and step in and save them.

They were given the opportunity to go down the road of truth, but they wouldn't take it.

One bit of evidence gave me a shock. It was a Brit. He said he was a sniper. He said he was up around the Derry Walls at that church, looking down into the Bogside, and he said he saw two men coming across at Joseph Place and going in a back door, one helping another, and that was me with Paddy Walsh helping me. He said he had the two of us lined up to shoot us. He followed us right up to the back door, and the reason he gave for not shooting us was because of the yellow card.

How little did we know there was a boy up there who had us two lined up and if he squeezed the trigger that was the two of us dead. To me, he was using the excuse of the yellow card, because he knew full well the yellow card never counted. They shot many a person in the North of Ireland that they wouldn't have if the yellow card had been adhered to. I think something just distracted him from shooting me and Paddy Walsh and then he used the yellow card to make out he was following the rules. But to be sitting there and a boy says he had you lined up and all he had to do was squeeze the trigger and the two of us were dead, that gives you a shivering you don't forget.

REGINA McKINNEY

We had been brought up to pray for people and I think we kind of got a shock when we found how laid-back and unrepentant the soldiers were. We felt insulted, not only by their actions but by their reactions, the way they spoke at the Inquiry, the way they looked at us.

Yes, I mean after 30 years we had already forgiven the soldiers, and we still have. But it was very hard to take. I just felt, 'How can they sit there and just not acknowledge it?' If they had even just said 'sorry', it would have meant a lot for us. They got an opportunity and didn't take it.

Mammy never got over it. It took 25 years for her to even start to come to terms with it. We all went to hear the evidence at certain times. Those particular soldiers who were in Glenfada, we all went to hear their evidence. It was hard on mammy, and hard on us all because she was there. You are watching her reactions and seeing it all over again. These men took away everything we had. We can discuss it now as adults. Getting married, having children – my brother had to give every one of us girls away. Five girls in the house. Things like that. Knowing that your children have no granda.

I grew up praying and believing that somewhere along the line these men are going to be fathers and grandfathers, that they can't go through their lives and not stop to think what they did in Derry, what they had taken away. But to see it not even acknowledged ... I was really shocked. I was very hurt by it.

I believe that a big mistake happened, that they really hadn't much of a choice and they didn't act on their own. I wouldn't hold them entirely responsible for the entire incident. But I do hold them responsible for the shooting, because men are men and know what they are doing. But in the immediate aftermath, the lies didn't come from the men, but from higher up, which made it doubly worse.

That was the other thing used to drive me crazy about Saville. He didn't mind so much the soldiers making remarks that would insult the families. But if the families laughed at any point – and it wasn't because something was hilarious but at the stupidity of the stuff that was coming out. I mean, how thick do they really think we Irish are? It is like watching a film. You laugh without realising. We weren't allowed those feelings. We were hush-hushed. There were times you had to laugh out of the sheer frustration and shock. My God! Here they are telling absolute and total lies. They say one thing and then the next minute say they don't remember. There was a complete lack of respect towards the families. We sat and listened. I remember one of them saying the bishop had guns up his cloak. And the way they made it out was like it was a battlefield. Well if that was the case they must have been facing very silly soldiers.

EILEEN GREEN

The killing was bad but the cover-up was worse. To see the extremes they went to .... You had General Ford, you had Captain Jackson, you had General Tuzo and Colonel Wilford. They were all there on the day and never saw nothing. I think that speaks for itself. I was there. I never saw anything but I heard shooting and saw people running. These were all intelligent men and in Derry at the same time and they neither seen nor heard anything.

JOHNNY CAMPBELL

The deeper they went into their evidence, the bigger the hole they were digging. They had their stories all mixed up, and their stories were stupid. To me, the soldiers hadn't ever thought about it. They just did what they were told by other people smarter and a lot wiser than themselves. That's why they didn't have their stories straight. And they could hardly go in and tell the truth, anyway. They couldn't say, well, 'OK, it looks like I shot an innocent man, guilty as charged.' So I wasn't let down when I didn't hear what I wanted to hear.

The officers were a bit cuter, smarter. Reading over the transcripts, you could have picked a young fellow off the street and he could have done a better job in the witness box than the ordinary boys. Some of them were saying one thing and then contradicting themselves in the very next sentence. But that doesn't mean they are innocent. They knew they were being used. It was time for them to say put their hands up and they didn't do that. They had 30 years to think about it, and they still went in with lies and half-truths. I could have no sympathy for them at all. But the officers, and the civil servants and the intelligence agents, they were the boys who knew what it was all about.

In a way, the lies were worse than the actual shooting. Without the lies I might have forgiven them the shooting, coming up with stories the way they did, and holding their stories up for 30 years. They had all that time to say it and they didn't, that my father was no gunman.

Even at the Inquiry, they were trying to set the ball rolling again, saying that, 'OK, even if these people were innocent, we were under fire from other people and that's why it happened.' They just won't take blame.

When they came to my father's part, I was there every day, listening to every word, because this was very relevant to me and my life. Other days it was more general stuff and you could have gone to it or not. But when it was my father, it was my place to be there.

BERNARD GILMOUR

There was one soldier who said that he went in shooting mad. He was as hard to believe as the ones saying that they had done nothing. He came in with a Para tie on him, and wings. He wouldn't wear that every day of the week. This was in-your-face stuff. This bastard shot my brother in the back. When they showed him the photo he said, 'That's not the bloke I shot.' Then they said, 'You shot a boy through the neck,' and he says, 'That's right.' But he kept denying that he had shot my brother. And I felt like saying, 'Ye lying bastard.' Every one of the families had that same kind of experience. There were two girls in the front and they broke down one day and had to go out to get away from this soldier lying. The bastard probably gloated at seeing them girls crying. Not crying over 30 years ago, but crying over what he has just been saying. It was the worst photograph you could have seen – Barney McGuigan lying on the ground.

Barney McGuigan, with his wife, Bridie

And they were giving the medical thing about how the bullet had entered through his head and what it had done and all. I felt bad for them girls. This was a Scotch bloke that was in the tank unit. He was an arrogant wee bastard. Every one of them was arrogant.

I came the whole way from Derry over to London and stayed in a hotel to listen to someone behind a piece of hardwood. It was soul-destroying sometimes. They were the most important people to talk and you wanted to see the reaction on their faces.

The people who were killed were all murdered. The soldiers who did it should be prosecuted. But there they were gloating. They are living among English people as NCOs [non-commissioned officers] instead of being classified as murderers. But I don't think there'll ever be prosecutions. They'll say, 'Your family members were all totally innocent, and they were all shot by soldiers, but Hugh was standing beside an IRA man and we were shooting at him. And Barney McGuigan was standing beside an IRA man and we tried to fire at him and shot Barney.' All killed accidentally.

JEAN HEGARTY

I lived in Canada when Bloody Sunday happened. I was away for 30 years. Every time I heard mention of the Parachute Regiment, I associated it with the word 'elite'. But when they came to give their evidence they didn't live up to it. I thought one or two of them were OK, fairly intelligent people. I'm trying not to be derogatory but they were what you'd expect from regular soldiers. Can't get a job, don't seem to be all there.

I think officers are a different breed. Whether they go to schools that lead them in that direction, or because of their family background, they're army through and through. You can't understand them because you can't get inside their brain. None of them came out of that shell. All of them stayed in the mould of the officer class.

There was one soldier in particular whose life I remember thinking was horrendous. He obviously suffered from mental illness. Now I don't know if the mental illness was a result of Bloody Sunday or if he had it at the time, but he was certainly a victim. That one stood out.

I have no idea how whoever shot my brother was feeling when he was standing there pulling that trigger. I have no idea if I had've been standing in his shoes what I would've done. My views prior to the tribunal would have been that he was in a range from someone who was 18 years old and shit-scared to some psychopathic bastard of 30 who enjoyed it. But where in that range was he? And, if I had been in his shoes, where in that range would I have fallen?

To me, the bigger crime is when somebody like Mike Jackson stood there and lied through his teeth. Colonel Wilford, too. That's a bigger crime than events unfolding that you maybe don't have much control over. The only revenge I would care to take would be on the likes of them – the officer class. The worse crime is not that Kevin was killed, but that Kevin was killed and some bastard in a uniform doesn't give a shit that it happened.

Most people that I am involved with have their own opinion of Bloody Sunday and I don't think the evidence has changed it. I would like to think that I had something of an open mind. But I suppose my perception has changed. I'm no longer quite so liberal. I know they are not all seasoned psychopaths. But I know now there's very few at the shit-scared 18-year-old end of the spectrum either.

DAMIEN DONAGHEY

The soldier who shot me hadn't even the guts to turn around and look at me. At lunchtime, he had to walk past us. He couldn't even look at me. Some of the soldiers' statements were unbelievable. One soldier said he wouldn't drive the car Gerald Donaghey was in because he seen nail bombs but the boy that did drive the car said he saw no nail bombs. Like the man says, you don't have to be a rocket scientist to see the lies.

Like the soldier who said he fired 23 shots, 19 at the one window; you could even see barristers that represented other soldiers looking at him. But he has kept up that story for the last 30 years. How did he fire 19 shots at a window and the window didn't break? The soldier who shot me said he shot a bloke with blonde hair, 5'6", which couldn't be me. And then no one admitted to firing at Johnny Johnston, but he was shot too. No wonder they couldn't look at you, and us sitting there.

I was there from 7.30 the morning the soldier who shot me was giving evidence. I was there from the minute he walked in until the minute he walked out. If I am supposed to be the guilty one, why could he not look at me? He's saying I was a nail bomber and then he couldn't admit shooting me. He said he might have shot me instead of saying he did shoot me. Widgery said the two soldiers collaborated, and that me and Johnny Johnston were shot in the wrong. Even Widgery said that. But these boys, even until this day, couldn't turn around and say we had nothing in our hands. What can you do?

In every army, as far as I can see, there are the fall guys, and that's how stupid the soldiers who did the shooting were. It's the main men up the line who should be prosecuted, like Jackson and Heath. The government covered up everything before and after Bloody Sunday, saying they had no meetings when they had meetings. The ordinary soldiers, the paratroopers, stood by the commanding officers and the commanding officers, who are supposed to be educated men, hadn't a fucking clue. The soldiers are that stupid they stood by their officers but the officers did not stand by the soldiers.

Wilford was across from where Pilot's Row is now, standing against a wall in Glenfada Park watching his soldiers shooting people. So he had to be giving the orders. Wilford has never risen up the ranks since Bloody Sunday. He is still the same Colonel Wilford. Jackson was only an understudy to him then, but now Jackson is the top man for the whole British Army. If Wilford did everything right, why did he not get promoted to a major or whatever is the higher rank? He has stayed the same for 30 years. Everybody else has risen above him. He is the senior fall guy. He is that fucking stupid, he wouldn't or couldn't tell the truth, even to defend himself.

At the end up, I don't think we will get any of them prosecuted. One of the problems is that only some people had bullets in them they could trace to certain soldiers. With other soldiers, you couldn't trace them. I would love to get them prosecuted for the families of the dead. We are all right, the wounded, but the dead can't speak for themselves.

LIAM WRAY

When it came to the top army officers – Ford, McClelland, Steel and so on – it was pass the buck. You got a wee bit of the mindset of these people, the arrogance and the fear. The arrogance of their class, the fear that they are going to let the side down. There was a lot of that.

Much of the time, it was boring, the same blah-blah-blah. But after a month that frustration passed. Eventually it meant nothing. It wasn't even a spectacle.

Take the fella that murdered my brother. What he did on Bloody Sunday, he doesn't feel was wrong, because he was brought up in the system to see my brother as an enemy, somebody who had to be taught a lesson. It never was going to cause him a conscience problem, because they didn't see the victims of Bloody Sunday in the sense of having an equal humanity. There is something about the army that makes them all robotic. Maybe they think that is part of the deal of being a soldier in Her Majesty's service. You don't have feelings, you do your job.

There was another soldier that you couldn't help getting the impression was trying to be honest. This was a situation he didn't want to be in. There could have been a lot more killed and wounded, so there had to be a lot of decent soldiers in there, who must have said no. When you're a soldier in that situation, hearing so much gunfire, your natural thing is to be tense. If you're doing something against a civilian population and they react, the natural thing is to react back. I have always had to live with the fact that not all soldiers are bad boys.

There was frustration at their evidence and at the lack of incisiveness in the Tribunal. We had situations where you had people coming in alleging, 'I am a PR man for the 22nd Light Air Defence Regiment', but he was over in Glenfada Park in civvies and you know these boys are military intelligence. But the Inquiry accepted that they were PR men. Again it's the nature of the Inquiry. It's obvious they are well schooled and their evidence is presented in a way that makes it very hard to apportion the blame. There is never anything that was preplanned. It was seemingly all done on the hop.

PATRICK NASH

You wouldn't know where to put your rage. You would go home or back to the hotel and you wouldn't feel too well. You felt you had no redress. Maybe as young men they wouldn't think, but at middle age, you imagine they're going to feel some sorrow, but I didn't see any. We saw what I would call genuine sorrow maybe once or twice.

Who in their right mind would want to be sent here? Why did they join the army? It was an option for them to make a living. But you don't expect to be sent here. They were told before they were sent in, 'You're going to be fired on, there's going to be an awful gun battle, we are going to take some of these guys out.' Those guys came in prepared for a war and there was no war waiting for them. I'll tell you who was shooting at them – the boys at the other side of the Flats, the boy that fired 22 rounds and never even hit a wall, never mind a window. They heard their own guys shooting and just thought, 'This is it.' I think these guys were scared of what they believed was going to happen. It didn't happen, but it didn't stop them being frightened. Is that an excuse for killing people? No, I don't think so. Some of them might be victims because they're suffering. I suppose some of them are suffering still. I'm talking about the people who all went up there and said, 'I'm an alcoholic, I've been depressed.' How many are still suffering today?

Jackson told lies. He had to be brought back to explain the lies but it doesn't matter to these guys. The officers were far better prepared. That didn't stop you seeing through their lies, but they were better prepared.

Jackson's shot list was ripped apart in cross-examination. All these guys allegedly report in to him and tell him exactly where they were and exactly where the person they shot was and mark it down on a map. That's him. But none of them remembers reporting in to him or putting any references down on a map. And some of them couldn't have done because they were at Altnagelvin at that very time. They tried to land bodies at Altnagelvin and were told, 'No, we are too busy.' So they said they took the bodies away again. Where did they go? My brother was in there along with McDaid and Young. Where did they take them? What did they do with them? Why was that barricade sanitised? They lifted bodies from that barricade. There were bodies lying all over the place.

You begin to wonder if some of them are right in the head. There were blokes sending memos to one another about whether to put the Royal Navy into Lisahally and the Air Force on standby to bomb the Creggan. And then there was Ford talking of 'shoot the ringleaders'. Who's that? Someone who stands out in a crowd? Someone wearing a big yellow hat? The ringleaders of what?

I don't think the Inquiry was for us at all. It wasn't for Derry people, it wasn't for Ireland. I think that it was some type of an exercise that was done for Britain's world standing. I don't think they care about people as such. It's a whole lot of people playing little games in offices and getting paid for it.

And as much as we know the truth and what people giving evidence said, there were some soldiers I did feel told the truth, but most were of no help to us.

KAY DUDDY

I had an experience one time at one of the anniversary events when this guy approached me. I was talking at the event about my 17-year-old brother and I got very upset, so we took a time-out. The guy approached me and he said, 'I am sorry', and I said, 'I'm sorry for upsetting people, which we spend our lives doing.' He said, 'No, you don't understand. I used to serve here and I didn't know what we were putting you through. It didn't register with me.' You get the odd thing like that. There were some family members who got phone calls from soldiers asking for forgiveness and stuff. Personally it didn't happen to me, but for a couple of people it did. They managed to get their hands on phone numbers and phone in the middle of the night saying, 'I am sorry, forgive me.' They wouldn't say why they had to be forgiven. This happened long before the Inquiry.

MICKEY BRIDGE

I was totally focused on trying, through my lawyer, to put the soldiers in the position where it was quite blatant that they were lying. I got the

Mickey Bridge, 59, from the Creggan, one of nine children, a labourer on Derry docks, was shot and wounded as he walked into the open in the Rossville Flats car-park, remonstrating with the soldiers after they'd killed Jackie Duddy. Mickey Bridge is now married with four children and lives in the Ballymagroarty area of Derry.

The Bloody Sunday Inquiry

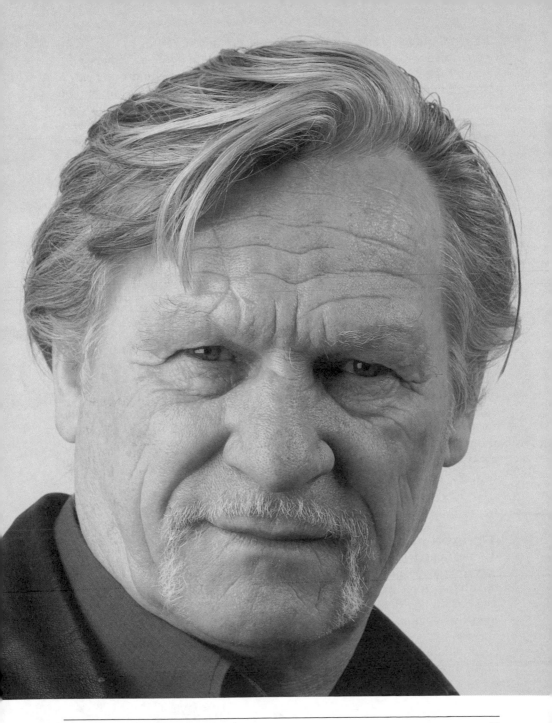

impression there was a couple of people getting hung out to dry. There were officers who were very well protected by the lawyers, others who weren't. There was one soldier there who clearly said he told lies in 1972. He said the statement he made back in 1972 was drawn up for him and he was told to sign it. That was glossed over at the Inquiry. In fact, his own side tried to discredit him. He was represented independently. There were one or two others who also said the statement they gave back in 1972 was constructed for them and all they did was sign it and it was not true. There was no elaboration of that.

To say that the soldiers were lying is a statement of fact. In the Flats car park where I was shot, we are dealing with an open space and a distance of a maximum of 20 yards in broad daylight. They didn't see a man lying on the ground, or a group of people gathered around him, nor two men running out. Mickey Bradley may have been in among people when he was shot. But I was in among nobody. I was out in the open. And they all swore they didn't see me. I must have been totally invisible or they must have been totally blind. Christopher Clarke summed it up well. If none of the soldiers giving evidence shot us, some other soldier must have, because there is no doubt we were shot by soldiers. But not only did none of them admit to shooting us, none of them bore witness against any of the others. That portrays a stance which Saville should have addressed. If a number of them are guilty of murder and attempted murder, which they are, then the rest of them are just as guilty of covering up, of being accessories. The fact that they were all anonymous made it more comfortable for them in doing that. Giving them anonymity didn't help to bring out the truth. It was a factor in the cover up. Saville had the power to take away anonymity and recommend prosecutions if soldiers were lying, but he never did that.

JIMMY DUDDY

Personally I have changed over the last five years, after watching the hearings. If there could be convictions, it wouldn't matter to me if a man served a day in jail. I want to see the man who killed Johnny in a court without all the protection that he had in the Inquiry, without being able to hide in a box. In the Methodist Hall in England, the complete arrogance of this man was obvious, the complete denial and the lying, even when Arthur Harvey ripped him to ribbons. He just would not concede. I changed. I began to think, 'Maybe a day in court would do you no harm, boy. Let me hear you speak like that when you could be facing five years in jail. Let me see you then, taking the attitude of, I can't remember, I forget, I don't recall.'

When the Inquiry was announced, a lot of us had great hope that through the passage of time these men would all be family men and have grandchildren and that remorse would have dug into a few of them. But it wasn't to be.

Some of them wore their Paratrooper ties or had their emblems on. One of them, who was a shooter and an animal, wore a white t-shirt so we could see his Paratrooper tattoos around his arms: 'brotherhood' and all written all over them. He blatantly was showing these, boasting if you like. That came out very strong to me from the soldiers.

The man that shot Johnnie was brave enough to shoot a 59-year-old, and his mate shot a 15-year-old, but he wasn't brave enough to sit in the security of the Methodist Hall in sight and of me and the rest of the families.

There was a lot of the non-paratroop soldiers who did try to tell the truth. Listening to them, they were ashamed of what had happened. Some of them would have carried visions in their head of seeing terrible things being done, not by their regiment but their army, maybe suddenly seeing what other soldiers, 18- or 19-year-olds, could do and get away with. It shocked them.

Some of them got a fair whacking by the army team because their evidence wasn't what was wanted. They tried to make them out liars, although their evidence coincided with all the other evidence.

One of the soldiers who gave his evidence would have been at the Essex factory in Bligh's Lane in a local post, and had seen the march going by and had a powerful pair of binoculars. He saw the soldiers moving into Rossville Street and he stated that one of the soldiers ran across the waste ground firing his rifle from the hip. He said he just couldn't believe it because the soldier was doing something that they were trained never to do, because firing like that you could shoot anybody. The army legal team went at him like vultures, trying to make him out a liar and throwing up photographs supposed to show that he couldn't have seen this at all.

But at the end, Clarke or somebody put up a photograph which was taken by a RUC man, Sergeant Brown, who actually came in from behind the army and had a privileged position to see what was happening. He didn't get any of the actual shooting but his photographs showed who was in and who was where, and it had a time-line too. One of his photographs showed you the corner of Glenfada and you could see Essex up above in the background, which proved your man was telling the truth. He had a clear view. Fair play to that soldier. He was going against the grain in telling the truth, and the army lawyers tried to destroy him. He confirmed what a lot of civilian witnesses had already told the Inquiry. You could feel his genuine sincerity. He was probably 50 years of age.

JOE MAHON

I wasn't even called to the Widgery Tribunal. I was in hospital. I remember two policemen coming in. One was a wee fat detective and I said then that I had seen a man getting shot by a soldier, and the policeman said to my father, 'It would be better if that boy said nothing at all.' That was it. I was never called to Widgery.

Some people say they know which paratrooper shot them, but I don't know which one shot me. The bullet that hit me went through the hipbone and into my stomach and out and lodged in the other hipbone. It was a hot pain in my stomach. I thought that I was hit by a rubber bullet but Willie McKinney was lying beside me there in Glenfada Park. I was on the footpath and he was on the road beside me and he said to me that me and him were hit. I couldn't understand. I looked at him out of the corner of my eye. Jim Wray was lying about 10 feet in front of me. I was going to get up and try to run because I didn't know I was shot. I could hear the paratroopers shouting behind me. It wasn't until they had finished arresting the people that they came across the car park and I was going to get up and run but I heard a woman's voice say, 'No, no, son, lie still son, let on you're dead.' I went back afterwards to thank the woman but I never found her. I lay there as if I was dead. Jim Wray was lying just in front of

Joe Mahon (right and far right), now 49, was shot and wounded as he fled from soldiers in Glenfada Park. Joe Mahon is a construction worker and father of five and lives with his partner in the Shantallow area of Derry.

me as the paratrooper walked past me. I could see his feet walking as he came up to the back of Jim Wray's feet to get through the gap. Jim Wray kind of moved his shoulders. He didn't move his legs. The lawyers at the Inquiry tried to trick me. They said, 'Did he move his legs?' He couldn't have moved his legs because of the wounds. He just moved his shoulders. Then the boy went bang-bang twice in the back. They said they only found one bullet hole but I saw his coat rising twice. I feel guilty for not calling to him when I saw him moving to tell him to pretend he was dead.

I'm glad that I picked the para out in his civvies. I'm glad they showed me that photograph of him. Even though he is dead, they can say, 'Right, that's the soldier who murdered Jim Wray.' They walked past Willie McKinney, they walked past me, never looked at the ground for weapons, never looked for nothing, up to Jim Wray, shot him and walked on past him. The first thing a soldier would do was try to recover weapons if he believed there were weapons. But I wasn't touched and Willie McKinney wasn't touched. I could have had a gun, even been lying on top of it.

People say they were high on drugs, but not that para. I picked him out in the video as he was going back into Abbey Park by himself, out of sight of the other paratroopers, which isn't a done thing either.

He went there himself through that alleyway and he apparently shot Gerard McKinney and Gerald Donaghey in there. He came back in again, stood over Jim Wray. This is the second time he has passed me and Willie McKinney and Jim Wray. He took his helmet off and I saw the blond hair then, the black through the blond hair, and he kept his helmet off then and he was on his own. The other paratrooper was across the far end of the square but he couldn't see him when he passed.

Then I heard the voice say, 'We've got another one.' Then, 'We're pulling out, Dave.' They walked past me and again never searched me, never searched Jim Wray, never searched Willie McKinney. It seemed a wild long time. It might have only been up to a minute, but it seemed a wild long time.

What scared me the most wasn't the paratrooper. It was the silence. I couldn't hear a car, couldn't hear a bird, you know, everyday sounds. I couldn't hear nothing. I turned round to see where he was then. He was half to three-quarters way across the square and he got down on one knee. Again he had the rifle towards me and I mind just turning my head away looking at the fence waiting to be shot again, or waiting to be shot, because at the time I didn't know I was shot already. I thought that this was it now. I saw him bending down and taking aim and just then Eibhlin Lafferty, who was to become my wife – she's my ex-wife now – came around the corner and called, 'Don't shoot, First Aid.'

People say he did fire and people say he didn't fire. According to her, a bullet went through her trouser leg, so he did fire. But that was probably the last bullet he had. Only for her coming he might have finished me off, but he wasn't a bit worried. He just walked back. He just walked away and I saw him looking back. I turned my head away. I lay there and I felt a hand on my shoulder and thought it was them lifting me, but then I heard a Derry voice. They carried me into the house.

They took me into the house and I sat down on the sofa. There was a nurse in the house and she cleared out the room and she opened my trousers and saw the bullet hole. The minute I saw the bullet hole, I was in shock. They started taking the combat jacket off me and took the jumper off me too. They were arguing whether to send me to Letterkenny Hospital or else Altnagelvin and my friends said, 'No, he's going to Altnagelvin.' Just by chance, there was an ambulance that was leaving. I think it must have been Mickey Kelly and someone else in it. They put me on the floor. My head was towards the driver and I was looking out the back doors, you know, the black glass you can see out of but you can't see in. I remember seeing the red brick houses on Bond's Hill. I mind going to the hospital and the policeman standing there. He probably thought that he was doing right, and pushed a wheelchair over towards the ambulance for me. The ambulance man lifted it and threw the wheelchair away.

I mind the whole bed shaking. According to a nurse, they couldn't find a pulse. I could hear everything, but I couldn't make contact. The first thing I knew I was getting cut here, cut there, then this nurse found a pulse and they stuck a needle up my arm and they cut my leg and cut the clothes off me.

Not one of the soldiers admitted any of this happened when they gave their evidence. But I was lying there and watched it happening. I saw it. I didn't need their evidence.

It doesn't matter that that soldier is dead. I want the truth to come out that Jim Wray was murdered. A wounded man shot in the back. Murder. That's what I want the Inquiry to say. I want them to use the truthful word, murder.

I want to say also that the paras did not take over the Bogside on Bloody Sunday. They came in as far as the Flats, then they stopped. They might have fired into the Bogside but there were no paratroopers at Free Derry Corner, none in Meenan Park or Dove Gardens, none in Creggan. I remember a map of all the places people were shot, and you could draw a straight line where everyone was when they were hit. An imaginary line from Fahan Street right down. Everyone was shot in a straight line. There was a pattern to it. Wee things like that still annoy me.

When you think back over all the evidence and everything that's come out, it's hard to remember that before Bloody Sunday it was a pantomime. We went out on a Saturday and Sunday and we threw stones at the soldiers. If they caught you they would've given you a kicking and let you go again. Then we used to go up William Street and swim in the swimming baths. We used to fire stones down the Lower Road. There were boys standing down the Lower Road and we knew them by first names because every Saturday and Sunday they were there. When we started throwing stones at them they called us back by our first names. But after Bloody Sunday everything changed. This was real now, this was real.

ALANA BURKE

S ome of the time I felt like getting up and punching the face of the soldiers giving evidence. There was an awful feeling from the soldiers behind screens. I felt, 'Go on, show us your face, let us see you.' They were like cowards behind a wall. I was there when Jackson gave evidence. Our legal team just tore him and high-ups like him to bits. They lifted lumps out of them. It was quite evident one was covering for the other and it was all a pack of lies.

A lot of times when you were sitting there, you couldn't say anything, you couldn't react. A lot of the times people just got up and walked out. There were times we broke down and started laughing. The whole place was in an uproar from some of the statements they were coming out with. They were ridiculous.

A lot of the times it was so sad. You were sitting in floods of tears for the families it was relevant to, whoever the relative was that this particular soldier was connected to. You know that they could sit and say, 'I'm looking at somebody who murdered my brother, I'm looking at somebody who murdered my father.' It was absolutely awful.

I think that the officers didn't really want to take responsibility for giving instructions to soldiers, because they would have been left to carry the can. They were cowards. Whoever gave the order to bring them in should be taking responsibility for what they did. But at the end of the day, only one person can pull a trigger. They were not under any danger whatsoever.

I wasn't in London the time the soldier connected to me gave evidence because I was sick in hospital. I took a nervous breakdown. After all that waiting, all that length of time, I couldn't be there. Disappointment wouldn't be the word to describe how I felt. Because of the impact that the injury had on my life, I wanted to see this man, I wanted him to realise what he had done, even though what he had done probably seemed insignificant to him. And for a long time I felt too, and maybe I still do feel, that it was insignificant because I wasn't shot but was hit by an armoured vehicle. But the impact on my life was colossal. It really destroyed me, and I wanted to be there. After all that time waiting, I wasn't.

But at least he accepted responsibility and he accepts liability, so that was a big thing for me. It gave me a little bit of closure. My life's just been a mess since it happened, with one thing or another.

JOHN KELLY

We were promised an open, transparent inquiry, a public enquiry, but that wasn't the case when the gagging orders, the Public Interest Immunity certificates, came in, when the screening came in and so on. Some soldiers behind screens, RUC behind screens, no evidence that was risky to the 'public interest'. The public definition of the Inquiry just disappeared.

The week the soldier who killed my brother gave evidence, there were 130 family members in London to listen. It was the largest contingent that went over. You couldn't take your eyes off him. We had seen photographs of him from 1972. But to see him now in physical form for the first time was dramatic. We had his statement from beforehand. You could see in that he claimed 80 odd times that he didn't recall or did not remember. Now that's a guy we believe murdered at least four that day and injured others, and he didn't recall anything about it! He didn't remember shooting Michael, he didn't remember shooting Paddy Doherty or Barney McGuigan and possibly Willie McKinney. Michael Mansfield stood up and got him to more or less admit that there was a possibility he could have killed Barney McGuigan. That was really, really powerful for the McGuigan family; that they heard for the first time out of this guy's mouth that he could have shot their father, husband. But the most powerful part was when Christopher Clarke stood up for the tribunal and read him the allegations against him. I was shaking, not being nervous but from pure emotion. When Clarke asked him if he had anything to say, he just said, 'No.' I think it boils down to the fact that he knows he'll be protected no matter what's proven against him.

There are soldiers, too, who would be alive today if it hadn't been for Bloody Sunday. Look at 18 paras blown up at Warrenpoint in 1979. Would that have happened if Bloody Sunday hadn't happened? The paras that came into Derry on Bloody Sunday were not just responsible for 14 deaths, they were responsible for a lot of deaths and injuries afterwards, to soldiers as well as civilians on all sides. The paras, all those years later, had an opportunity to put some respect into the British Army by telling the truth of what happened on Bloody Sunday, but they didn't take the opportunity.

When F was giving his evidence, I'm saying, 'Mickey give me strength to get through this', because it's hard to be in the same room as the man you know has murdered your brother. The night before, and even in the morning before we left the hotel to go to listen to that evidence, I got down on my knees and I prayed to Mickey and I prayed to Padre Pio and to Our Lord to give me the strength to get through it. I'm not just about Mickey, I'm about everybody, and I would say to Mickey, 'Give everybody the strength to get through this.' Don't get me wrong, I don't believe in ghosts or anything like that, or spirits floating around the place, but I do believe that somewhere Mickey is looking down on us, especially myself and the rest of my family, and he has done well so far I think. Many a day I had doubts whether I should carry on. Last night I was lying in my bed saying, 'I'm fucked off, I think I'll go and get another job.' I'm saying to myself I should be doing more, but I don't know what to do. I'm sure Mickey will direct me and tell me. I depend on the people I am working for, and I'm not working for the Trust, I'm not working for the families, I'm working for the dead and injured. That's the way I've always looked at things. That's the way I am. It's about achieving what we set out to achieve and we are not there yet. If we do walk away with satisfaction, I will throw the words back on Sergeant O's face and say, 'It was a job well done.' I remember that expression when he was asked about the killings on television. He said it was a job well done.

7 Neighbours

KAY DUDDY

God love them. For everybody that went into that Guildhall, this was the chance that they had been waiting on for all those years. What we found amazing was how many people hadn't talked about it, couldn't talk about it, and now had the chance to tell their story. When they spoke, you could see them back there in the Bogside. You could see them crunched down, dodging the bullets. You could see them running. Then, in giving evidence, they had to talk in terms of being north-east of this situation or south-west of that situation. This was the precision that the representatives of the soldiers expected civilian witnesses to have. You could see people telling their story and you could see in their eyes that they were back there, hiding behind that telephone box, pulling themselves across to the laneway by their elbows. And the soldiers' lawyers wanted to know, 'Was that north-east?' or 'Could you just look at that map there and tell me ....'

I had an experience with one person who came forward. I met this person on the street afterwards and I thanked him for allowing himself to be grilled and he started to cry. He said he was a coward because he ran. I said, 'You were no coward. If you hadn't run that day, you would have been one of the ones we are talking about in there.' The impression I had was that the poor man felt that I had given him permission to forgive himself. I would say a lot of the civilians in there could be suffering from survival guilt and didn't know it. They probably still don't know it. So the very fact that they got a chance to tell their story will hopefully let them leave it now that they have dealt with it. They were very helpful to the families. But they needed to come forward for themselves, too.

EILEEN GREEN

You could feel sorry for people because some of them could express themselves better than others. The lawyers on the soldiers' side could see people's weaknesses and they would jump at them and make them nervous. You have to remember, too, that it might have been the first time some ever spoke about it. People had never been through anything like that. Bishop Daly, he was marvellous. Martin McGuinness did his best giving evidence on what happened on the day, but they didn't seem to be interested in that. They were more interested in other things. People could only come and give what they saw on the day. I think that's all they should have been asked.

JIMMY DUDDY

When you go through it, it brings it all back to life and you don't realise it. I've seen in a lot of the civilian witnesses that they were reliving it. Bloody Sunday had 27 victims, but I would say you also had nine or ten thousand that were traumatised and the Inquiry brought it all back for them.

One of the Knights of Malta girls was hit with a rubber bullet. Glasgow gave her a grilling over where exactly she was at that instant. When she put an X on a map, it could have been 20 or 30 yards out. She would have been less used to maps than the legal teams were. She was left crying from them trying to make her out a liar. And Glasgow must have known she was telling the truth.

Even in my own evidence, I had difficulty. OK, it was my own fault for not physically going round the route to re-memorise it to myself. You think you know it but you don't. Until that day I gave my evidence, I didn't look at any photographs. I just went on my memories of the day. I didn't realise until then I must have seen Barney McGuigan dead as well as Paddy Doherty, because I bonded the two of them together. I visualised Paddy with blood all around his head, which isn't the way it was. I could see from the photographs it wasn't.

I must have walked on down and seen Barney as well and the blood from his head. There was still shooting going on. You just don't absorb it. I would have been by the wee plinth where the Bloody Sunday memorial is now, and the bullets were rushing over it and hitting it.

I should have been more ready, but I didn't expect the badgering when I was describing it as best I was able. They put maps in front of you. I wasn't used to it. I didn't have a computer then. I found the north, south, east and west business very confusing. The legal teams who weren't from Derry and only knew it from maps and photographs had their minds orientated to north, south, east and west. When we talked about coming from Creggan, if you were thinking of Rossville Street or

William Street it was in front of you. The Brandywell was to your right, the Strand Road was to your left and the Guildhall was further in front of you. To someone coming from the Waterside, Creggan is in front of them, the Strand Road is to the right and the Brandywell is to the left. They were pestering me on the direction the shooting was coming from. It's very hard under pressure to orientate your brain like that. I think they were trying to trick me. Glasgow was an arrogant pig of a man.

There were a few civilians out of 800 or 900 witnesses who wouldn't have seen things and then said they did. They had seen things maybe days before or days after and tied them in with Bloody Sunday, and that would have had a detrimental affect on the truth. They were trying their best to tell the truth. But evidence from photos and other witnesses showed they'd mixed things up with another day.

JEAN HEGARTY

I still don't have a clear picture from the civilian evidence whether Kevin was shot as he got to the door or as he was going through the door. But I can't blame anyone for that. Ninety-nine per cent of the civilian evidence

Jean Hegarty (originally McElhinney: photo overleaf) was one of a family of five and five years older than her brother, Kevin (second from left above), 17, a shop worker, shot dead as he crawled along Rossville Street away from the soldiers. Now 55, married and a mother of two, she lives in Pennyburn. Jean Hegarty works part-time on a voluntary basis as administrator of the Bloody Sunday Trust.

Jean Hegarty

The Bloody Sunday Inquiry

came from people trying to do their best. There were a few who certainly did try to make themselves important. But there wasn't too much of that.

Even if there was an element of people perhaps not telling the full truth out of communal solidarity or so as not to help the soldiers' case, I don't necessarily think anybody lied – depending on your definition of a lie. I think there may have been things that people didn't mention. Maybe they didn't tell the full truth. But, really, there was no reason to hide anything.

MICHAEL McKINNEY

There was one man who came in who was asked to name an IRA man. He was in a bad way. I think he gave the name. He was an honest man wanting to do his best. It was unfair to ask some witnesses to name IRA members. It put them under a lot of stress. I know that, because myself and John were working with them. I think there were a few, true enough, who came in to play to the gallery. And a few who didn't take the whole thing seriously. But they were just a few.

JOHNNY CAMPBELL

Some of the civilian evidence was very good, but it has to be admitted there were some people just putting themselves into places where they couldn't have been. Overall, it was good. Listening to it was a very personal experience. You were hearing about other victims and their

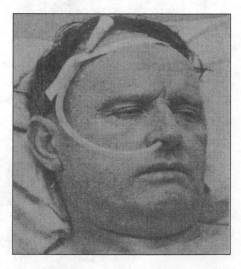

Johnny Campbell (photo overleaf) was 22 on Bloody Sunday, one of a family of nine children living in the Creggan. Their father Patrick (left), 51, a docker, was shot in the back and wounded as he tried to find shelter at Joseph Place. He died in 1984. Johnny Campbell is now a mobile shop-keeper and lives in the Creggan with his wife and five children.

Johnny Campbell

stories, thinking what their families were going through. It was pretty gruesome at times, but it brought the experience together. I learned bits and pieces about individual victims on the day, about people who were heroes and people doing horrific things. I learned the names of people I didn't know before, and that there were people I knew there on the day that I wasn't conscious of. It was an eye opener at times. All these bits and pieces of stories that had developed on their own, some of them came out and I could piece the whole thing better. Before, we had sketches and a whole lot of spaces. Some of the spaces were filled in through the Inquiry.

GERALDINE DOHERTY

I think our civilian witnesses did really well. They had to face all that number of lawyers and judges, and the public and the families watching and listening to them. I'm not sure I could have done it. All that responsibility …. The one I remember most was my uncle's best friend, Dennis, or Donnacha. I wasn't sure he was going to get through it. He was filled with distress. He'd been with Gerald on the march and they got lost from one another half way through. I remember Leo Young, too. He was with him the whole way, but I was always afraid to ask Leo what it was like, what Gerald was like in the back of the car. Did he say anything? Was he able to speak? I didn't realise until I heard it from Leo that my uncle was alive in the back of the car. They pulled Mr Rogan and Leo Young out of the car and arrested them, and then the soldier at the checkpoint got into the car and drove it to the barracks. That was the whole story that we got through the evidence. They were standing around poking at my uncle's body, staring in and making a laugh of him, and then taking him to a car park outside the barracks and doing an explosives test. I thought: my uncle is lying wounded in that car. They should have automatically let the car by. They pulled the blanket off and moved his body and planted the nail bombs and put him back in. My Uncle Gerald, having his trousers unzipped, and them ones having a laugh. I thought then, 'Oh, ye will meet your maker some day, too, for what goes around comes around.' I get angry and annoyed and really hurt when I think about it, that they could let someone die like that. It's not normal. An ordinary human being would try to save another person's life. Maybe he could have lived. Maybe he would still be living now.

MICKEY BRIDGE

Some people went in to make their statements to the Inquiry solicitors with a great naivety. They set out to make a statement that was acceptable to themselves and also to the Inquiry. They went in with an assumption, 'I am going in here and I am going to tell my truth.' When it came to giving evidence, their truth was dissected word for word, and the Inquiry used both their first draft and their finished statement, which Saville said at the start he wouldn't do. He changed that.

Saville also decided to address rumour, second-hand information and hearsay. I objected to that and a few other people objected also. That situation applied only to the civilian population. It applied to people, some of whom should never have given evidence at all. Thirty years ago, in a place like Derry, sometimes rumour became fact or it was broadened and elaborated on. I know at least one person who gave evidence who wasn't even there on Bloody Sunday.

But those rules of Saville couldn't apply to someone who had got anonymity. They couldn't apply to the soldiers. If I was a soldier and you had been my friend for 30 years, the chances are I would have talked to you about Bloody Sunday. Unless I tell you that I was to give evidence, because I have anonymity you don't know, and I could go up there and tell a totally different version to what I was telling you. Even if you did discover this was happening and tried to give evidence, you wouldn't be allowed to because you would be breaking the anonymity. So in practice, the procedures Saville put in place applied to one section of the community, to civilians giving evidence. You could use hearsay to challenge civilian evidence, but you couldn't put hearsay in to contradict the soldiers.

There was one person gave evidence who said I was in his mother's house drinking tea on the day and then we went directly to William Street where we were rioting. There was a selection of photographs of me on the march that put me in certain places at certain times, and they totally contradicted what the man said. He was absolutely convinced this happened. Let's put it this way – he made it up one time and he has been telling the story for so long that now he really believes it himself. After I was shot, if every person that said they gave me a hand, helped me into the house, they would have been fighting to get a touch of me, but some of them are convinced it happened. It didn't happen.

So some of those people who gave wrong evidence were genuine. Then there were people who played to the crowd. A businessman went up there and he gave evidence about a conversation he had with the Derry RUC Chief Lagan in 1972. Someone should have asked him why he didn't bring that out away back at the time of Widgery. He was playing to the gallery.

There were Derry people who attended the Inquiry for as long as I did but didn't have any input into it at all. They had a need to have their experience addressed as well as I had. A lot of people were very upset about what happened at the hearings in the Guildhall. Bloody Sunday didn't just affect people like me and the rest of the families. It affected literally the whole fucking town, because if you weren't shot or one of your family wasn't shot, you knew the people who were.

PATSY McDAID

I was a witness myself. They tell you that you are going to be nervous, but when you have nothing to hide there's nothing to it. You can relax, and sit there and tell what happened. You're not adding bits in or hiding bits out, nothing like what the Brits were doing. That's why they were all muddled and tangled up. But I was confident. I knew what happened that day. I could go through the whole lot every time, no bother to me, because there it is and always will be.

As a rule, the civilians went up and told what they saw, although some of them were very confusing themselves. There's people that said they carried me into an ambulance, but nobody carried me anywhere. I found afterwards that it was Paddy Walsh that came to me when I was shot. It was Paddy Walsh that was behind me and said, 'You're shot in the back,' and I said, 'No I'm not.' I didn't know I was shot. Then, panic stations. It was him that told me to go into a house at Joseph's Place.

When I read people's evidence, I realised they must be mixing me up with Paddy Doherty, because Paddy was shot dead in the same area where I was hit. I think they were confusing the names, Patrick Doherty and Patrick McDaid. Nobody carried me anywhere. I was able to walk. I walked out to the ambulance. The first aid men helped me.

I never attended the hearings in the Guildhall. I get angry very easy. Even in England, you were sitting there biting your tongue. If you got up and let a roar, all the papers would have it splashed all over. You didn't want to take away from what was happening. That's why I never went near the Guildhall. I just read all the statements. When you did that, you could see it was only natural that they would try to find a way out. Some girl said she saw a guy up in a flat with a handgun. They jumped on that and tried to make a major thing of it. Same as that shooting in William Street. That's the things they're trying to play on. They had to try anything to get themselves off the hook.

MAURA YOUNG

There was a wee woman from Helen Street came on. Glasgow was asking her how far was it from Helen Street to William Street. She said,

'Och, son, sure it's only down the street.' He asked what she knew about the riots, she said to Saville, 'You see, mister, it's like this. The wee fellas go down and fire stones at the soldiers so the soldiers would fire rubber bullets back, and then they sold them to Americans, that was what the riot was about.' Saville looked in awe of her. But it was pure truth, she wasn't set up. You compare it with the soldiers. You knew they were schooled. The civilian witnesses took the stand and told what they knew, tried their best. None of this, 'I don't know, I can't remember.' Some of them were very emotional, having to go back and talk about seeing people dying. Glasgow asked another man about John Johnston, who was killed on William Street: 'How did you know Mr Johnston?' and he said, 'Well Mr Johnston worked in a tailor's shop and dressed like a solicitor.' When Glasgow asked him to explain, he said, 'Well, put it like this, he didn't get his coat out of Dunnes Stores.' Days like that broke the intensity.

LIAM WRAY

Some people came off the stand traumatised. They'd thought they were coming up to tell their story and that they had nothing to hide. But they were made to feel as if they were liars. Saville and his two cohorts were meant to represent the interest of civilians, but they didn't do a great job on that. The story we were getting from our lawyers was that there was nothing they could do as they represented the families, not the Derry civilians. I told my solicitor I wanted him on his feet challenging what was happening. So my legal team got up and got egg on their face, but to the Wray family it was important that they challenged Lord Saville on that. That was the beauty of having a legal team to represent your view.

Some of it was amazing and heartfelt, some of it was off the wall. Obviously, some people over the years had memories implanted in them. It was something a few of us became aware of early on, and it was worrying.

Going on my own experience, I only have about three vivid memories of the day. There's a lot I don't remember, and that's caused me problems over the years. I watched people giving evidence who were able to recall everything from the moment they left the house to go up to Creggan, who they met and what they said. I thought, 'Either I am defective or these people are brilliant.' I discovered afterwards that when people were giving their statements to the Inquiry's solicitors – I am not sure if it was intentional – when they had blanks they were being told, 'Well, you were at William Street, you said', and shown photographs. Basically, they were encouraged to have memories that they didn't really have. This wasn't helpful when they came to give evidence. I think people were so eager to tell the truth they didn't see the importance of being pedantic. They went up there in the belief that they had nothing to hide and weren't under scrutiny, they were just witnesses. But some of them were either cut to shreds or badly hurt. They were trying to give honest evidence, but there was trickery being used against them.

When we talk about young fellas who rioted, we don't see them as Derry young hooligans or thugs. They were seen by the people, especially in 1969, 1970, 1971 and 1972, as the protectors of their area keeping the thugs out – the British Army, B specials, UDR [Ulster Defence Regiment], RUC, depending on the year. But when you watched Saville's face, or Hoyt's or Toohey's, when a witness said, 'Aye I threw stones', it was as if they were looking at dirt on their shoe. They didn't have the mindset to understand, they were coming from a strictly law-and-order point of view. So from day one, some civilians were poor witnesses because the tribunal saw them as law-breakers. I don't think the tribunal was showing impartiality at that stage. The vast majority of people who threw stones in 1969 are pillars of society now, teachers, social workers and whatnot. I don't think the Inquiry ever managed to cast off that mindset and see those civilian witnesses the way they were seen in Derry.

CAROLINE O'DONNELL

Some of it was good, some of it was bad, some of it was madness. There were older people, maybe a bit senile, who couldn't recall what happened. You couldn't stop laughing. They were away with the fairies. You were thinking that this was a total waste of everybody's time. But most people went up and told the truth. Some people did play to the crowd. Some had to stop because they were crying and had to leave the hall. They were bringing up stuff they probably thought that they had dealt with years ago but they hadn't, especially people that had seen somebody being shot in front of them or beside them. I must say the majority of the civilians went up and told the truth, because that's all they could say about it.

DAMIEN DONAGHEY

Some people went there to glorify themselves. Like the woman in the Brandywell who said she saw weapons at 5.30 that night. Why say things which weren't true? And there are others like her. One man said he was at a wake of a relation when a boy came in and took a gun and nail bombs off him and hid them down the toilet, which was total garbage. Nobody else in the room saw it. A few people tried to make themselves out bigger than they were. But the vast majority were there to tell the truth of what they saw. I think the people of Derry did well. I thank them for it. In the end, I don't think that there was much hidden – although the soldiers hid plenty.

KATE AND PATRICK NASH

*K*ate: There was good civilian evidence, but there were other parts that were exaggerated. If you listened to what everybody says about Bloody Sunday you would get the feeling there was half a million people on the march. Now only did everyone seem to be on it, but they all saw something important, and you know that wasn't the case. Over the years people have listened to other people in the pubs, watched programmes on

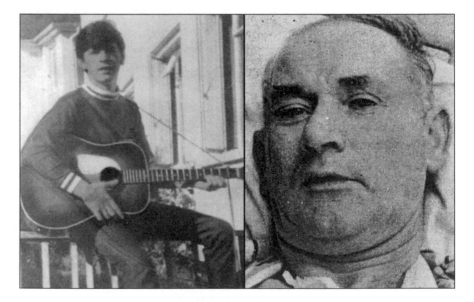

Patrick Nash, now 60, and **Kate**, 56 (both right), were the oldest boy and girl in a family of 13 living in Creggan on Bloody Sunday. They were brother and sister of William, 19 (left above), a docker, who was shot dead at the Rossville Street barricade. Their father, Alex, 51 (right above), also a docker, was shot and wounded when he went out from cover to comfort his dying son. Patrick is a widower and father of four, Kate a divorced mother of one. Patrick and Kate Nash both now live in the Creggan.

The Bloody Sunday Inquiry

TV and read newspapers and their memories were distorted. I don't know whether some of them believed what they were saying.

I don't believe there were many who would have withheld things through a sense of loyalty to us or loyalty to Ireland or maybe to make the soldiers look bad.

*P*at: Some can't separate fact from fiction. But you know the genuine witnesses, the people who still have the memory with them. You can tell just sitting listening to them explaining themselves. You can tell that they are still hurting because of what they saw that was just not right and it has stuck with them. In the same way, you could pick out the ones that were exaggerating. The woman who saw the gunman in Glenfada, then moved up to Barry Street and was able to see stuff that happened there. She moved then down to the Brandywell and she saw a car full of guns. This was just totally impossible.

They thought they were doing a good turn, but the families requested that if they were going to go and give their evidence, give it all, warts and all. It's no good us seeking the truth from the army without seeking it from other people as well. So we asked for everybody to go in there and give a true record of what they could remember. The truth, just let it out. People withheld stuff. It was obvious they didn't want to answer, for whatever reason, and that's a false thing. If someone was afraid to say something that might help the army's case, the army had already done enough damage to warrant whatever's coming to them.

ALANA BURKE

I was drawn back all the time. I wanted to be there as much as I could. I used to leave the wee boy to school in the morning and come straight into the Inquiry and spend the day there. You couldn't do that every day, obviously. I wanted to hear everything. Some of it was painful to hear and some of it was devastating. Some if it made you angry. There were the times you felt very, very proud of how strong people were and how much they could remember, especially older people after such a length of time, that they could come on a stand and be word perfect and they remembered every detail exactly the way it was 30 years earlier.

There were times you heard evidence you didn't like, didn't want to hear. Some of it was bordering on the ridiculous, but I think everybody came together as much as possible.

Giving evidence myself was the end of a long road of wanting to tell what I saw to the world. For a long, long time, I had closed what happened deep inside me. Nobody could get near me. I wanted to talk about it, but at the same time I couldn't, because if I brought it to the front of my mind, I couldn't cope. I had been very young at the time. I thought, 'Can I go through this big Inquiry and tell it exactly the way it was and be able to cope?'

As it gathered momentum, I kept saying to myself, 'Aye, you can do this. When it comes your time you are going to be able to cope.' But when it did come my time, I didn't. I thought that giving evidence would have brought me a wee bit of closure inside. But on the stand I went to pieces completely. I couldn't recall what I wanted to without it being hurtful, it was paining me, and it still does. It will never go away.

BERNARD GILMOUR

O ne or two of the civilian witnesses really exaggerated. A lot of them told stories that would have been impossible to happen. But it was what they remembered after talking about it so long. And you can't fault them. You can't say, 'You're lying.' They were wanting to help the families. They got their memories, maybe, from sitting in a bar and somebody telling about something and them saying later, 'God, I mind that.' But what they remembered was somebody saying it. It was nerve-wracking. Some people broke down. There was a girl that was with my young brother when he was shot dead, and she stayed with him until he died, and then she saw Barney McGuigan getting hit. And she had to tell what he was saying before he died, with the family all sitting there. She was only a young girl of 17 at the time.

8 IRA

GERALDINE DOHERTY

I was in total shock when I saw some of the IRA witnesses. I was pleased they came in and gave evidence because if they hadn't the Brits would have said, 'Well, there you are, they must have done something they don't want to admit to, and it must have been something really serious.' But they went in there and gave their evidence and it was obvious they didn't do anything. The reason I was shocked was who they were. I saw some of them getting on the stand and I thought, 'Naw! Him! I don't believe it, your man there in such and such.' You don't know, do you?

JOHNNY CAMPBELL

I think the IRA should have come forward earlier, but I can understand their position too. It was a touchy subject, but I have no bother with that side of things because I know that they weren't involved. I thought the Officials were very honest in admitting to what they did. That's all you can be expected to be, I suppose – honest.

PATRICK NASH

I had the feeling the Provisional IRA would come forward. It doesn't matter when they came forward; I respect them for the fact that they did come forward. If they hadn't, it would have looked like they had something to hide. Martin McGuinness went up on the stand and you knew he was telling the truth. He refused to give the names of other people, even if he knew the names, even if they had already revealed themselves. He was honest himself when he said, 'Yes, I was a member of the IRA. Yes, I was second in command and I left the Provisional Movement in 1974.' Now there is probably other stuff he could have told them, but would it have been relevant to us?

The Official IRA should have never been in the position they were in on that day and I was angry at that. They did not seem to have any notion about the danger they were putting people in. They admitted themselves that they had a weapon there in Colmcille Court and that they fired in retaliation. But that admission had to come because of other evidence, other civilian evidence. I don't think they had any option but admit it. And the reason they gave for not having the rifle removed earlier was unbelievable – that they went down the day before and there seemed to be too much activity and they were frightened off, so they waited until 10,000 people came down William Street and then went in and lifted it. Come on!

JEAN HEGARTY

I was very disappointed that they came forward at a very late stage. I don't believe that any of them lied – depending on your definition of a lie. But I felt some of them didn't do the day justice or themselves justice or their organisation justice. One or two of them were OK, but some of them I just felt were unbelievable. I felt that they were tailoring their evidence.

I was glad the Official IRA admitted to having fired shots. Everybody knows that they did, so what was the big deal about keeping it a secret? But as for their explanation of how they happened to have a gun at the ready just at the beginning, I'm not sure. So, they didn't move the guns on Saturday night because they had a bad feeling. Now, I can live with that. I'm a big believer in feelings. I can believe two guys came down from Creggan on a Saturday night, took the guns out and then said, 'No, this doesn't feel right', and put them back where they were hidden. But I can't buy that they came down to the Bogside on Sunday when the march was about to arrive and the place is surrounded by soldiers and they thought that this is a better time to do it. I mean, that's a load of crap.

EILEEN GREEN

You have to remember the Brits had a very bad reputation for fighting the truth. You have to remember how devious they were. I suppose people were just watching the Inquiry to see how it was going to go, if it was worth giving evidence to. I think when they saw how well it was run it gave them the incentive to come. They knew that's what the families wanted. They sat back for a while to see if these British people were serious about the truth, and then they came in.

REGINA McKINNEY

The only one I remember from the Provisional IRA was Martin McGuinness. It was the day the media all arrived, and I thought, 'Here we go.' I mean, I'm not into him. I've nothing against him, either, but I'm not into him. I thought, 'What on earth are they doing? They are ripping this fella apart.' They were going into everything he ever did in his whole life. He should have been just treated like everybody else. What had his life story got to do with Bloody Sunday? That was the one day I got sick. I was in the bathroom more times, I was so annoyed.

At the end of the day, the Official IRA jeopardised people's lives. They played their part in what happened. But I still have to say they didn't kill anybody. I'm not saying I am in agreement with them, because I am not. They shouldn't have been there with anything. It was a civil rights march. My father's life was put at risk because of all the circumstances. So all the circumstances should be shown up. And if I'm able to turn round and say that about someone who is from, like, 'my side', then I also expect the other side of the fence, the British side, to stand up. Whatever their roles on the day, those who did stand forward were in their own way brave. It meant they were going to be seen. I don't have respect for them, but I appreciate them giving their evidence. By the same token, I have less respect for the soldiers. To me, their evidence was cowardice and lies. They keep trying to place the blame on the IRA, but the guns that shot my father and the rest were not fired by Irish men but by English men.

MICHAEL McKINNEY

Some time before the Inquiry moved to London, the question of the IRA coming forward came up at a Trust meeting. I think everybody knew the IRA had to come into it one way or another. Angela Hegarty suggested that John and myself should make the approaches. So we had a number of meetings with Martin McGuinness and other prominent Republicans, and we put across the solidarity of the families in wanting the IRA to come forward. Outside of those meetings, there would have been other contact. It was a bit of a process. It went on for a while. There was coming and going. Their first reaction was, 'Leave it with us, we'll come back to you.' Eventually, word came back that they'd be sending five people in. As we know now, there were more than five.

It was important that the IRA would have an input in order to put to rest the Brits' allegation of a gun battle. We all knew there had been no gun battle. But I'd been of the opinion from the start that the IRA would have to take the sting out of the allegation. We were conscious that, if they didn't, the Brits' lawyers would probably judicially review the Report. They'd have said, 'You can't publish this, because you don't have all the evidence for your findings.'

I was very much aware of the difficulty Republicans would have, knowing their history and tradition, their lack of trust in the British, the fact that they are, after all, a secret army. I'm sure it was a hard decision for them. As far as I am aware, there was no precedent for them to step forward like that.

The evidence they did give tied in with the solid block of civilian evidence. The civilians who said they saw gunmen were very few, and the main thing is that, even if you take it on the soldiers' evidence, none of those gunmen were engaged by the soldiers. There was no gun battle.

We all knew the Official IRA fired shots. But they were never identified as targets by the army. Those shots played no part in making Bloody Sunday happen. There was the shot the Officials admitted from Colmcille Court at ten to four, which hit the drainpipe. But there were no shots fired back at that man. Instead, Soldiers A and B fired and hit John Johnston and Damien Donaghey and swore blind they were bombers. In fact, if you listened to the evidence of Wilford, those Official shots had nothing to do with the paras coming in. At ten to four, Wilford was already dead set on going into the Bogside anyway. He was pulling his hair out to get in.

DAMIEN DONAGHEY

I think the IRA had to come in at the end up because there were people like Paddy Ward, who told total lies about IRA actions on the day. He said he went into a house and fired a shot out the back yard. I live next door to that house. It was fucking lies. He may as well have said he was Rambo. He wanted to boast about what a big man he was in the IRA, which he'd claimed in Johnston and Clarke's book about Martin McGuinness. That's all he had to say to Saville.

I knew Eddie Dobbins well, who was in the movement at the time. He told me 18 months before the IRA witnesses appeared that he would definitely give a statement. I went to Madden & Finucane and they took a statement off him. But then they said they couldn't represent him because they were representing us. So he got that solicitor from Belfast, the fellow who represented Martin McGuinness, and gave his evidence to him. It was held back for whatever reason until near the end. But there were always people like him who were going to come forward. Of course, a couple didn't come forward.

I knew that the Official IRA had fired shots even before the fella gave evidence. He came to me and told me he fired a shot after I was shot. Everybody knew at that time. It was not hidden over the years. It was common knowledge in Derry. Saville and the barristers of the army tried to make it out far worse than it was. The Official IRA men admitted firing the shots. One of them became known over the years as 'Bishop Daly's gunman'.

I never even heard the shot that was supposed to have hit the drainpipe. They were supposed to have fired it before I was shot but the man who fired it told me it was after I was shot. After that, I never heard anything. Me and John Johnston were taken to a house and, to be truthful, I knew nothing about Bloody Sunday until the next day and saw it on the TV. We were shot nearly half an hour before everybody else. I didn't know half the people were dead. I saw people being brought in wounded, Danny McGowan and other people, but I never knew there were so many dead. I have never heard much about other shots. I know Mickey Doherty, God rest him, fired a shot later.

MICKEY BRIDGE

The IRA gave selective evidence. They were right to come forward because the fact that they hadn't was being used as a big stick to beat the truth with. Them coming forward took away the excuse that they were hiding something. But in the process of appearing they broadened the remit. Saville's original position was he would address Bloody Sunday itself and maybe slightly before and maybe slightly after. But some lawyers seemed to want a full history of the IRA with details that had nothing to do with Bloody Sunday.

There's a possibility other shots were fired apart from the Colmcille Court shot and Father Daly's gunman, but going on knowledge within the town, there wasn't. There were people at the Inquiry who said they saw this, saw that, saw everything. There's been evidence there since 1972. The Inquiry used statements of, 'I have been told this …' or 'I heard that … ' to broaden itself out. They drew a chart at the Inquiry and put gunmen in it, at least 20 in the vicinity. But the shots from the back of the flats and the shots from William Street are the only confirmed IRA shots even now, and they came not before the paras' shots but while people were getting shot.

JOHN KELLY

It took a lot of work and a long time to get them in. Saville had turned round and said that if they didn't come in the impression would be that they had something to hide. That was the most powerful argument. You have to remember that the reason they gave evidence was for us. We pushed them. We put them on the line in that once they gave evidence the public would realise that this guy or that guy was an IRA man, which for them was a lot of risk. We didn't want people to tell lies, even if some people might have thought that would be doing us a good turn. The IRA came in and played their part. That was vitally important.

We always knew about the Sticky [Official IRA member] who shot at William Street and about Bishop Daly's gunman. It was important that the Officials told their story and how they remembered it. I can only take their evidence at face value. Whether they were telling the truth is not up to us to judge. We asked them to tell the truth. It was a massive thing to see them there, for the first time ever prepared to sit in front of an English tribunal as ex-IRA men and tell their stories. They really put themselves out on a limb. A lot of people might have known about the shots being fired but didn't realise who these guys were. I have nothing but praise for them. A lot of them had got on with their lives and put all that behind them. But they came forward for us. The Provisional IRA, too.

ALANA BURKE

I f the legal teams for the soldiers had anybody up on the stand that was in any way connected with the Provisional IRA, they gave them a really hard time. There were people who were maybe on the periphery of the Republican movement and would've known individuals who might have been involved. The lawyers took them to pieces and rubbished their evidence because they thought that they were connected with the Provos or the Stickies.

Everybody knew about the Officials shooting, so it wasn't a surprise. The Official IRA had to go up on the stand and hold their hands up and say, 'Aye, we did', because people knew they did.

MAURA YOUNG

I couldn't understand why the Provisionals waited so long. Why did they not put up their hands at the start and say that they were on the ground but that they didn't fire any shots? I was glad they came in the end because you have to hear everybody's side. There is no point holding back.

I believe that maybe if people had seen the IRA on the periphery after the event, when they were going home up the New Road or into Creggan or wherever, they might have thought, 'I am not mentioning that because what's the point, it has nothing to do with Bloody Sunday.' There were so many dead on the day, it was pretty obvious you'd see IRA men on the scene by the time it was through. But the events were over at that stage. So I don't think there was anything of significance that was held back by any civilian witnesses.

If they did hold things back, it was futile, because no soldiers gave evidence that indicated gunmen. It's been shown beyond doubt that the gunmen the soldiers claimed they shot weren't gunmen. There was no evidence from soldiers to identify actual gunmen. It was a few civilians who came to the Inquiry, 20–30 witnesses at most, and said they had seen civilian gunmen of one type or other. By the looks of it, most of them were identifying the same couple of individuals.

Bishop Daly spoke about the gunman in the Rossville car park just after Jackie Duddy had been shot. That wasn't a shock. We knew about that from the start. We knew from about six months afterwards about what they call the 'drainpipe shot' at the beginning, from Colmcille Court. So we knew there had to be a gunman there. And I think it might have been pretty obvious in 1972 that there were a few people around carrying private firearms, that there were paramilitaries about the place. Derry is not a good place for keeping secrets.

I am surprised the IRA came forward at all. I honestly believe, from doing all the research I could, that the IRA didn't play a part on Bloody Sunday. So, as for IRA witnesses coming forward, what information could they give? Look at the way they were treated, the way their evidence was dealt with. I think the attitude was that if you are an IRA man, ipso facto you are a liar to boot. The soldiers' lawyers were gloating to have got IRA witnesses up there.

It is quite clear if you sat six years through the tribunal that particular soldiers fired at unarmed civilian targets. There is no evidence to suggest anything different. Making a big deal about getting IRA witnesses in was just to bring in the fact that the IRA were a force at the time and there could have been one or two of them about. Well, so what?

Bishop Daly told the tribunal he saw a man firing a weapon. The funny thing was, no soldier saw him.

CAROLINE O'DONNELL

I think maybe they waited so long because they wanted to protect the families.

Quite a lot of them came near the end and did tell the truth. I suppose they were frightened for themselves. Maybe they thought, 'We will come out of the Guildhall and get arrested.' At the end of the day, they came through for the families. I was there for a few at the end. They were shaking before they went in, in case they would say something the wrong way and the soldiers would cross-examine them and the whole thing would be totally twisted by some smart-arse. When they came out the sweat was beating off them. Fair play to them.

KAY DUDDY

I thought, 'You bastards. You have given them an excuse.' What the Official IRA did was wrong. But at the same time, our loved ones weren't the people firing those shots, or our wounded. That to me was so important. Half the population could have been armed that day. But that didn't mean our loved ones were part of that, because they weren't, and it was proved beyond a shadow of a doubt that they weren't.

9 London

JOHN KELLY

When we got to London we were shown nothing but respect. We couldn't foresee how we were going to be treated, but I can say now, for the duration of time we were in London, the families were treated with pure and utter respect. We started off with nine or ten people travelling, because people couldn't get off work and that sort of stuff. But then we had weeks with 30 to 40 people. The more people you had, the more you had to look after them. I was a family liaison worker and had to work with the Inquiry staff as well, and the Inquiry people did a brilliant job. The families were their first priority. Of course, we had a few wee problems. You had to try and foresee everything that might arise, as well as the problems you didn't think of. There were people who were unemployed. If they went to London, how would it affect their benefits? And stuff like that. You had difficulties with hotel accommodation, with people who had physical needs. They had to be sorted out. I had been in London once or twice before, but I didn't know my way around, so I was depending on other people. I think the families became closer during that time. There were people within the families I had never met before, but all of a sudden we were travelling to London and we started to get to know each other and confide in each other and enjoy each other. Some of them are the young 20 to 30-year-olds, coming along. This was another generation of the Bloody Sunday families we were beginning to work with, to know. We all became more of an entity in London.

Each family had their own time. Saville had divided up all the action on the day into sectors. There was Sector 1, Sector 2, Sector 3, 4 and 5, where each family's loved ones were murdered or they were injured, and it was important that there were people there to support that family and vice versa when it came to their turn. My turn was when Soldier F appeared.

We were in an environment we hadn't been in before. There was the possibility of the families moving among paras and paras moving among the families. We were standing at the door of the hall one day and Wilford walked passed us. That was some sensation. You could have had a head-case among us, and god knows what could have happened. You have to think about all this.

JOE MAHON

As far as I can see, in moving to London, Saville was just doing what he was told. I didn't go at all.

PATSY McDAID

I only went over to London a couple of times because I am afraid of flying. John Kelly said to me I should go as it was the soldiers that did the shooting and they were the ones I should want to hear. That was right.

The group that was over was very good to each other. All were equal. Gerry Duddy knew his way around London. He would have known what bus to get. We would have been lost without him. Then if you had any problems, John Kelly was there and Mickey McKinney was there and Jean was there. If you go somewhere that you were never in before, you feel out of place, but I never felt out of place. When I went over first, I thought: 'London! What's going to happen here?' But I found there was no bother. Even getting sorted out in the hotels, Jean would have looked after you.

When you're sitting up there listening to them boys and feeling angry, you would love to be able to shout: 'You're telling a pack of lies, tell the

Patsy McDaid, now 58 (contemporary photo overleaf), had just helped carry a previous casualty to safety when he was shot and wounded in the Rossville Flats car-park.

Patsy McDaid

The Bloody Sunday Inquiry

pigging truth!' But you know everybody around you is feeling the same and then you go down and you talk about things. If you were listening and you came out and were on your own, you wouldn't be feeling the best, because of all the anger inside you.

You went down to the family room and you talked about what the boy up the stairs was saying. You weren't cursing and shouting because you were all part of it together. And because we were new, everyone went out of their way to help us. After the hearing was over, Gerry took you around and showed you places. You might have thought he would have said, 'Ah, I've been up there and done that so many times', but no, he would just say, 'Are ye ready, come on, I'll take you up around.'

Sometimes, when you go to other places and there's a group already been there, you would feel left out because they are all together. That's what I felt it might be like when I went over. But in London, we were all one.

BERNARD GILMOUR

The thing about London was that you had to be there for whenever the soldier who killed your relative, like my brother, was on, but also for some of the other families as well. So I travelled back and forward. It was different in Derry, where you could try to fit it into your normal life, so that it became part of it. My wife went every day in Derry. Then I'd finish work we would sit and chat about the evidence of the day for an hour or an hour and a half. But to be in London wasn't part of normal life. It was a duty.

KEVIN McDAID

The way the Inquiry went, it was never really in our hands. But it was removed from us completely when it moved over to England. None of our family went to London. The thing had happened here. So we didn't feel it was our duty to go there to hear about it. They had had all their guarantees, that nobody would touch any of the soldiers if they came here. I remember Christopher Clarke standing at the corner of Rossville Street, Aggro Corner as they would call it, watching the filming of the *Bloody Sunday* film. And Saville and the other judges walked around the town freely unconcerned. They were in no danger. None of us went to London and none of us went down to watch the video link either. But I did read the daily transcript of the evidence.

The solders were in their own place. Their names weren't given. Some of them we weren't allowed to see, even if you'd been there. How could we even be certain they were who they said they were? Was Soldier F really Soldier F? It could have been his brother. It could have been anybody.

JIMMY DUDDY

I could see the camaraderie when we were sitting around at the airport, in wee groups because of the size of the tables. In the evenings people would have sat about and chatted and have one or two pints, and that released the tensions of the Inquiry. Other times, we would have started codding about and telling jokes. Big Gerry Duddy was great for all that. There was great togetherness with big Mary and Mrs Doherty and him taking them around London.

I was never in London before, but over the years I would have met a lot of English people and my perception of them was that they were just nice English people. Then there are rotten English people. Just as there's nice Irish and rotten Irish. Certain parts of England are more like us, Geordies and Liverpool with their humour. And I found people in London very pleasant.

We were staying at the Dolphin Hotel and the ex-RUC chief constable was staying there, too. He had no security or flakjacket, no weapon or nothing, sitting having a meal. He knew who we were, and some of the families actually chatted to him in the evenings. I would have been courteous walking past. Here was a man heavily involved in the conflict, head of the RUC and obviously involved with the Special Branch, staying in the same building as us. How farcical that made the reason we were in England. This man would have been an absolute top ten target for assassination, and he was completely happy to be in our presence and trust. There were hundreds of other hotels in that area that he could move to, but he didn't. There was no reason.

ALANA BURKE

The first journey to London was horrendous. With practice it got better. By the time we got to the hotel we were exhausted and everybody was hyped up because we were going to the heart of Westminster, into this Methodist Hall, starting an inquiry into something that happened 30 years ago. We were riding on the wave of 'Look how far we've come, England's got to sit up and listen to what their army did in Northern Ireland.'

There was exhilaration going into Methodist Hall for the first time and finding your feet, wondering what way the Inquiry would operate, would we be allowed to go out and in as we did in the Guildhall? We complained about the security. They were over the top. I think because we were Irish, they looked on us like we almost had to be stripped naked to get in. We went and gave off stink to security, saying we weren't having it. There was one particular woman at the security belt when we were going through who treated us like shit. But they relaxed as time went on. I suppose it's all down to the English trying to make the Irish feel inferior. That's the impression I got.

So, initially I felt that we were in an alien land, but this changed. It was just finding your feet really.

My first reaction when I heard it was being moved to London had been, 'How are we going to manage that? How are we going to fix up for our children being looked after?' But everybody wanted to be there.

Everybody was living in the same place. Not everybody was completely happy all of the time. Sometimes things went wrong, but all these things had to be overcome because there were more important things happening everyday. Once you went to the Inquiry on a Monday morning, you looked forward to going back the next day, and you couldn't leave. It was riveting. You had to stay. When you made the time to go to London, it was only right that you should stay there for the four days of the evidence that week.

We had a laugh too. We use to sit and go over: 'What did you think of your man saying that?' and 'Wasn't that really ridiculous?' It was your whole life, really.

I was aware from the beginning that it was a huge event and I wanted to involve my two boys. My oldest boy went on his own. He's a law student at Queens and he was really into it because he did it as part of A-level Irish history. He was totally tuned in. I wanted to make a point of taking them to London so that they would remember. The youngest boy was able to write about it in his journal the next day and the teacher got him up to explain to the class why he was in London with his mammy and what happened to his mammy. I had never spoken to the younger boy about Bloody Sunday until I decided to take them to London. Then I told him.

I went over to do one of the commemorations in London. I think it was the first time a woman had spoken. There were all these politicians sitting beside me on this forum in some Irish centre. The women in the audience were horrified when I told them my story and came down and asked me questions about it afterwards. And I thought that is what the problem is – English people didn't know the human aspect of it and the after-effect of what happened. It is wee things like that that make them sit up and take notice. Whereas those English papers, they are just trying to protect their politicians, their soldiers, their government. From a human and a personal perspective, there were English people who couldn't believe what had happened and how it affected me and the other wounded. The wounded are living testimony to what happened. So I don't take at face value anything they print in the English papers.

LIAM WRAY

I didn't think it would do my mentality or my health any good so I made that decision that I wouldn't go.

Saville knew that Derry would have been all right but the High Court overruled him. That made him look good to the Derry people. But the truth is, he knew from day one it was never going to happen. In the end, I don't think it made a difference to their evidence. Maybe it was better, because now they can't claim intimidation or pressure or stress. The key thing is, everything was set up to suit and accommodate the military.

JOHNNY CAMPBELL

The lot of us were all working, which is the main reason we didn't go to London. Also, I didn't agree with it being taken to London in the first place, so I decided I was happy enough to follow it from here. If I hadn't been working, I suppose I would have been away myself because I think the British government thought if they moved it to London no one would bother going over. But they went over in big numbers and they had support from different groups over there. Overall, that was the right thing to do.

JEAN HEGARTY

Once it was clear that it was going to move to London, I was prepared to quit my job to go back and forth to London because I don't mind travelling and I had the ability to do it. I had no family ties. My husband was at home anyway. It was something I could do without it being a huge sacrifice. To tell the truth, if I'd been spending 24 hours a day with my husband I probably would be divorced by now. So, in some respects it wasn't all a bad thing. And I missed the big city. I wasn't all that long back from Canada and it satisfied a need in me. There was no hardship. I don't think it was the same in all cases.

Moving to London changed the dynamics. We became more of a family, and like a family had our good days and bad days. The group that travelled to London, the regulars shall we call them, gelled really well.

The soldiers were always going to use the excuse that they were under threat to justify not coming to Derry. Going to London was like calling their bluff.

I wouldn't regard England as an alien country. I had no fears about going there. My brother lives there and my granny lives there.

For me personally, London was good times. I made the best of a bad situation. We were generally finished up about 3 o'clock, 3.30. So I chose to make the best of the free time, to enjoy London and what it had to offer – the shopping, the theatre, the sights, museums, art galleries.

There were certain people in London we could rely on, the family liaison workers were there and there was another family member who had lived in London for a while and was a huge asset. We hadn't realised he knew it so well. But there was nobody you thought you could depend on that didn't come through for us.

MAURA YOUNG

I went once to London. I didn't like it. I was very weary. It is OK when you are on home ground, you can come home and bang the walls and shout, whereas there you were in the Inquiry, which was so intense, and then back to the hotel. I felt England was very hostile, that everybody was looking at us.

REGINA McKINNEY

For me, London was something of a journey. I remember sitting on the bus the very first day. I was nervous. I was looking at everybody and thinking, 'Fourteen men dead … all these families are together because of that.' We wouldn't have known each other if it hadn't been for all these men dead. There were some that I knew and looked up to – the Duddys and John Kelly and Alana Burke and the ones that had been wounded. It did me the world of good going there and being with them.

The tribunal itself, it was a very good learning experience. You learned what it was all about – other than the fact that it was about my daddy. You learned other people's views, even how the soldiers thought. As children you just assume that people will grow up and wise up. You teach your own children from when they are no height to say sorry. And here you see these grown men who are really like bad children, bullies. I have children. You bring them up to admit when they are wrong and to try to curb their anger. It was sad to see grown men acting like children that couldn't be corrected. That was a learning experience.

I was keeping myself in check, not letting myself go. The big thing for me was not to let my daddy down. I am standing here in London in the middle of the tribunal and thinking, 'I'm here to prove that my father is innocent, so that my family would be seen as an extension of his innocence, and that not only are we proud of him but that he would be proud of us.' If it was clear that he had no involvement, then it would be clear that we had no involvement. I would not have anybody having reason to look down on us. I'm not going to have my father accused of something and have us all tarred with the one brush. Us standing for what we are pulls my daddy into it. That's the way we were brought up, from before he died.

For me, family is before soldiers, Saville, government. This is a family that loved a father who was innocent and a family who are themselves innocent. That meant I couldn't allow myself to get angry or bitter. I'm not saying you don't be angry. The thing is not to release it, or lash out. You have to stop and think what you are here for. A lot of the families helped, even families that had to go through worse.

MICHAEL McKINNEY

I always believed that that evidence should've been heard in Derry. It was outrageous that we had to travel to London. But once we made the move, it was OK.

Initially a lot of us felt like we were going to a hostile country. Then we got into the centre of London, and people were pleasant.

I remember long before the Inquiry being over for a couple of weekends in Leicester and I found myself talking to people who you could have brought here to Derry and taken them into a bar in the Bogside and they wouldn't have looked out of place. The working class in England are no different to us.

I thought that the support that we got from the Irish over there was fantastic. It wasn't a situation where you had hundreds coming to the Inquiry. But there was a number never missed a day. They ran functions for us and they turned out faithfully and they were altogether fantastic.

CAROLINE O'DONNELL

My daughters came to London once and absolutely loved it – the questioning and cross-examination, everything. They couldn't get enough of it.

Caroline O'Donnell

Caroline O'Donnell (photo previous page) was 13, from a family of six living in Foyle Hill in the Creggan, when her father, Patrick (left), then 41, was shot and wounded in Glenfada Park. A city council worker, Caroline O'Donnell is a divorced mother of two, living in the Kingsfort area of Derry.

The first morning, there was a press conference in the Houses of Parliament. Then, we had to meet the Irish ambassador who invited us for drinks and a buffet one evening. A number of times, we were invited out to Camden Town, where there is a large Irish community. You didn't want to let anybody down so we would come back mentally and physically exhausted.

At the start, I thought it was a disgrace that we had to go to London. I knew I wouldn't to be able to go a lot. When you work full time, you can't. It was very awkward trying to get annual leave to coincide with the times the soldier who shot my father was giving evidence. It started in September and I went then, but I didn't go back until the following June as I wanted to keep some of my leave until when my father's sector was coming up. The Inquiry staff were fantastic. You just had to call up and everything was arranged, even taxis to the airport. You got this white envelope with your name on it with your flight itinerary, your bus ticket, and your train ticket for coming back, the whole schedule of who was up to give evidence that week, which hotel, whether you were full board or half board, smoking or non-smoking. All done before you went.

I also looked on it as a great holiday because it was free. One time we stayed in this new hotel. Because of who was giving evidence, a lot of people were over, so we all couldn't fit into the Dolphin Square Hotel in Pimlico. We were in these big suites. A massive bedroom with a double king-size bed and a huge shining bathroom with a shower and a bath, absolutely gorgeous, then a big living room, and a kitchen and another massive bedroom with another en-suite bathroom. You had the facilities there to cook if you wanted to. It was up to you to choose whether you wanted to take the £22 a day to feed yourself or go full board. The first time we went, we went full board, but then we found it tied us down. Any time after that we went bed-and-breakfast.

My daughters Amy and Caitlin went because Amy always wanted to see London. And she loved the Inquiry, got hooked on it.

When we were over together we treated it like a holiday, but because the Inquiry was there it was serious as well. I really enjoyed even the security staff going in. I enjoyed being friendly with them. There was one night we went out, and two of the security came with us. We became really friendly and they never looked at you like, 'There's the Irish coming over here and questioning our soldiers.' Any of the ones we talked to were very sympathetic. I think they were sitting in listening to the evidence and knew the soldiers were lying. Some days, if the Inquiry finished early because a witness phoned in sick or whatever, we would go to some of the bars in the area where it was all English people, and even in these bars they would have been over asking, 'How are you getting on?' You have to give credit where it is due.

We went out every night with the solicitors and barristers. They knew all the best bars, live music, good restaurants. We went to Soho a lot of nights as a group, all the families, solicitors and barristers, because they had fantastic restaurants there. For the barristers and solicitors, the Inquiry was their life during the day, but they went out every night. The crack was 90.

It changed my mind about London and people in it, big time. I was only ever in London when I was 14 and I was always afraid of it. I used to think, I don't like it, it's too English. But I grew to love it. I loved meeting the people. It was a learning experience. It is a fantastic city.

I still think the soldiers should have been made to come to the Guildhall. But in hindsight it's great that we had the opportunity to go to London.

KATE AND PATRICK NASH

*K*ate: If someone wanted to take a look at Harrods, Gerry Duddy would have taken them. He was like a tour guide. It was terrific to have that because London is a big city, and can be frightening if you don't know it. There were a few family members afraid to leave the hotel for the first six months. They found out six months down the line that there was nothing to be afraid of. They thought they were in dangerous territory, but it turned out they weren't. I personally didn't feel like that, but then I had lived in London for eleven years when I was younger.

Jean was very dependable person. There was so much light at her door. She was a tower of strength,

The public gallery was nearly always empty. Maybe it wasn't very well advertised. There was a general lack of interest. The English are not a friendly people. I know I can't say that in general because it would be stupid to think that a whole nation would be all unfriendly. I reckon in any big city people are just in too much of a rush to stop and think. London people get on with their lives and are not interested in what happened in a wee corner of Ireland. They are not interested whether their army or their government was to blame. They just don't want to hear it.

It was very hurtful to our family that newspapers were going on about all the money it was costing, how we could fly in and out when we wanted, living a life of luxury. I consider my home a hell of a lot more comfortable than any hotel, no matter how expensive. It had just furniture. It had none of the things that you love to have close to you, your photographs, the things you put on your walls, your own delft, your own cutlery.

*P*atrick: Charlie McMenamin used to take me outside. There was a green outside and there were days I couldn't get any lower. I mind him taking me out: we sat down on this wall and he sat and talked to me for three or four hours. It was only afterwards I noticed he wasn't talking at all. It was me doing all the talking, he was sitting listening. But you always felt better. He'd always seem to do the right thing. During my period in London, my son had a serious brain haemorrhage and my wife died and without the support of people like John Kelly and Jean Hegarty and Carol McAdams and Charlie McMenamin, I wouldn't have got through it. I wouldn't be here now.

I didn't know Gerry Duddy before I went. Some of the things I had been told about Gerry just didn't weigh up. That's why I changed my mind about the whole Bloody Sunday Trust. Over that period, he acted differently from what I was led to believe. He was one gentleman. If I ever go back on the drink I will buy that man a pint. And Jean Hegarty, although I was acting the wack with her, was terrific. I don't know how she did it, week after week.

MICKEY BRIDGE

The families let themselves down by attending the Inquiry in London after soldiers were allowed to give their evidence from behind screens. I wouldn't sit to see screenings because it was counterproductive. It was about the soldiers protecting their personal lives from publicity, not protecting themselves from harm. One person screened in London was the soldier who was a member of the SAS and fired the first shot that hit Damien Donaghey. I wanted the families to walk out but they chose not to. How they can justify that to themselves is beyond me. I would not under any circumstances go and sit and look at screened evidence from the person who probably started Bloody Sunday. He got immunity and anonymity – and then they put him behind a screen.

What was noticeable when the intelligence agents took the stand was not lies but the lack of evidence. Most of it was censored 'in the public interest' if it was any way controversial. Or they'd just turn round and say, 'I am not allowed to answer that.' The more you listened, the greater awareness you had that what you were listening to was a pack of lies.

TERESA McGOWAN

I was sorry I didn't go earlier. I only went once towards the end and I got a great sense of relaxation. It took the tension out of me. The reason I didn't go before was because of Danny's sickness. I thought, what if anything happened to him when I was away. But then, when it came to the last time, I mentioned it to my daughters and they said they would go with me. The other one came to look after her father. Danny was glad I went, in his heart. He never showed emotion, but he was glad I went.

I couldn't get over it. I thought it was fantastic, the way the solicitors did their job, and the barristers. It was very emotional too. The first thing I thought was that I regretted I didn't come earlier. I suppose when you have a person sick, a man especially, you put them in front of you.

My main concern would have been that Danny wouldn't have been able to cope. He needed to have somebody there with him. He couldn't eat, so his food had to be blended and nobody had the patience for it only myself.

When I got to London, I thought this was the greatest, I couldn't explain it to anybody. I got peace of mind coming to London. It was like a sense of freedom. I was thinking, why the heck was I so uptight about going away? I had a big family. I am sure they could have looked after Danny.

I went out when we finished at the Inquiry. We always went round all the shops and up to Covent Garden and across the bridges over the

Thames. That magician boy was in the box under a bridge when we were there. I couldn't get over that. I thought it was beautiful. It was near Westminster. The Houses of Parliament were gorgeous. I suppose all parts of London wouldn't have been as lovely as the part we were in, but I was amazed. I couldn't get over the hotel, having your food handed to you. It took pressure off me because I had Danny through his first cancer and then he got over that. But he was never well really, not 100 per cent. Then he took sick again and it was leukaemia, so he just didn't fight it. That break away was great for me. Danny was grand about it. I think he realised I was going for so many days and I would be back at the end of that time. As long as he knew I would only be away for those days, I think that consoled him.

GERALDINE DOHERTY

I had never been in London before. I only spent the one week there, for my Uncle Gerald's evidence. I felt very isolated. It felt like a very strange country, so I kept myself to myself. I went into the Inquiry and came back and sat on my own and thought about it. As the week went on I couldn't wait to get home. I was lost. I didn't know how the other family members were able to do that week after week. I thought London people were different people completely. Maybe not so much London people as the atmosphere around that building, the way you were searched when you went in, as if you were going to be carrying something, and then seeing the soldiers on the stand and the way they spoke. It was a disgrace. I thought, I will never come back here, never. And I never did. I was so angry and emotional, I wanted to cry. But I thought to myself, 'No, you can't let yourself down here in this room of people. We have to show that we are strong. If you want to cry, go back to your hotel room and cry all you like.' So that's what I did. Maybe the reason, too, was that I was on my own. I didn't have another family member with me. It had to be either me or my mother. There's me and a younger sister and an older brother and they don't get involved at all, so really it's just me and my mother. My sister has named her wee boy Gerald and she would be on some of the marches, but her and my brother wouldn't be into this as much as I would. So, really, it was just me and my mother who could have gone to London for that week, and it was me.

KAY DUDDY

It was like having a job. You got up in the morning, you had your breakfast and you went to Central Hall. You came back in the evening, you had a bite to eat and you farted about and went to bed. It wasn't you had to be there, it was you wanted to be there. I was there as much as was humanly possible. If we had to go to London, we had to go to London. End of story. It was just another hurdle to be overcome.

If Bloody Sunday had happened in Liverpool or Manchester, would they have brought it to Derry to hear the proceedings? I don't think so. It should have been in Derry all the way.

Going to London the first few times was like going into the unknown. Prior to that, I was in London once or twice in my life. Now, I never want to see it again as long as I live. I am sick looking at it. On the first day we were there, we laid the wreaths outside Westminster Abbey for all who had lost their lives as a result of the violence and there was a guy in a van and he called, 'Up the paras', or something to that effect. I have to be honest and say that's about the height of what reaction I remember. They couldn't have cared less if we were there for 13 years, let alone 13 months.

The Irish community helped us out big time. They invited us to events and organised nights out. I don't do that at home a lot. But when you are away you could be sitting in a pub just to pass the time. I didn't feel comfortable sitting in a pub because I didn't know who I was sitting with, or who would have been listening. I preferred to stay in. So whenever we were invited out by these groups who ran the Irish club, we felt you were out at home among people you could relax with. I mean, if you didn't relax you would go off your head altogether. But I was very selective about where I would relax.

It didn't change my opinion of the English because London is very cosmopolitan. It would be very hard to find a Londoner on the staff at the hotel. It was nearly all foreigners and they were lovely. As for actually meeting Londoners, it was nearly impossible, particularly in the area where the Inquiry was. There was Central Hall, Westminster Abbey and the Queen Elizabeth Conference Centre. Big Ben is literally around the corner. You walk up to the left and you're at Buckingham Palace. You were in the hub of where tourists come. What drew attention to us was the fact we had to stand outside to smoke and with us talking amongst ourselves there were sometimes people saying, 'Oh, is that an Irish accent I hear?' We met quite a few people that way.

I felt at the announcement of the Inquiry that we had taken on the British establishment and won. Then when we were in London, I saw this is where it all stemmed from. We were yards from Downing Street. We had brought it home to them.

EILEEN GREEN

England was tough. Me and my husband hardly got a night's sleep in it. We couldn't get used to the noise. And then you were up early in the morning. We would all have met at night time there and would have talked. That did bring the wider group together. Some families couldn't cope on the day when the guy who was supposed to have shot their brother or father, or whoever it was, was to say his piece. Everybody knew that one of the reasons we were there was for that sort of thing. We were all connected into the emotion. You knew that the others knew how you felt and vice versa.

My main fear was the underground, because of the threat from Al Qaida. Everybody was saying if they ever struck against London it would be the underground. I did go on it years ago when my son Patrick was in London. But not now. I'd hate to think we went through all that happened in 30 years and then came over to London to get blown up. That's the way I thought every day.

DAMIEN DONAGHEY

At the start, it was 100 miles an hour. You had Gerry Duddy, Jean Hegarty, Mickey McKinney, John Kelly and others who were over regularly and were able to take you places. After three or so times over, you knew yourself where to go, what buses or tubes to get. The Irish community in London were unbelievable, old Charlie, wee Danny and people like that. So, at the start I was a bit scared of London because I hadn't been there before. But I got used to it.

When we landed we were laying a wreath outside Westminster Abbey and a lorry passed and started calling, 'Stupid Irish bastards', but that was the only bad thing that we got over there. I thought with the paras up, there would have been more abuse. But there wasn't.

The Methodist Hall was an ideal spot. You had the Houses of Parliament a couple minutes walk away, Westminster Abbey was right there. There was a sense of taking the issue to the heart of the establishment. One thing that became plain was that people in London didn't really care. I mean that generally. You could be lying dead in the street and they would walk past you. You could be living beside people there for 20 years and wouldn't know who they were. It is a different culture. I couldn't live in it. It is too fast. But I didn't mind going over for four days at a time.

We shouldn't have had to go. They were able to come to the streets of Derry and kill and wound so many people. They should have had to come back. The talk about how they would have been shot was just a cover. We were probably in more harm over there, and I don't think, in the event, we were in much harm. The soldiers I saw giving evidence had five or six boys minding them. They would never have been touched.

Around Methodist Hall, there seemed to be a gathering of people every day of the week, going to Westminster Abbey and places like that. So we didn't stand out. I wouldn't be a great lover of the English, but from my experience now I could say nothing against them. People we met in the hotel and who worked behind the bar and in the restaurants, I couldn't say they were bad people.

10 Conclusion

BERNARD GILMOUR

I'm relieved that my mother and father didn't have to go through it. If they had had to sit in the Guildhall, with the photos coming up on the screen, and Hugh lying there, they would have died anyway. When they put that photograph up on the screen the first time, him covered in blood … I was looking down on him from the Flats when that happened. Hugh lying there dying and me standing there looking at him. I think about it all the time. And then it changes the way you think about other things. You would see them on the news, Iraq, Palestine, Afghanistan, and you would think about them. And you'd say, 'That's what happened to us. There, look. That's exactly what happened to us. It's happening to them people now.'

PATSY McDAID

The Brits shot innocent protestors in the street on a peaceful march in India. Not one of the civilians was armed when they marched up towards this army place. I forget the name of the army boy who was in charge at that place. He lined his soldiers up and told them to open fire. He killed over 400.

It was the same policy in Iran, where the Shah's army was being advised by Brits. When the protesters came down the street, they opened fire, killing so many. But it blew up on them.

If you go back to the 17th century, workers in England were on strike and marched into a town where the Brits were all around at the windows waiting for them. They said that one person opened fire on them so the army fired back, killing so many again.

That's the way I look at Bloody Sunday. This old story about the IRA is all rubbish. They saw the marches getting bigger so what they did was try to scare them off the streets. They are the most devious crowd in the world to work with when it comes to politics. Bloody Sunday to me was not an attempt to bring out the IRA, it was a policy to put people off the streets. But people still came out. It was the same in India. The people still marched.

March on. You have to battle on to highlight throughout the world that the Brits have lied again. We've been doing it for over 30 years, marching every anniversary for the truth. We can keep on until the truth comes.

ALANA BURKE

I'd be very tuned in to world events, but that comes from my mum. She was a great activist, a civil rights woman. She worked for the Nationalist Party for a long, long time. She then progressed into working for Sinn Fein for a while. She was more a Nationalist than a Republican. She was on all the civil rights marches, Duke Street, Burntollet, Magilligan, a fantastic lady, and made us very aware from when we were young. That is probably where my son gets it from. He is doing a law degree and would be very politically aware.

Before the Inquiry I might have accepted things I saw on TV, but not now. When Bloody Sunday happened the British were saying, 'They were terrorists, they were holding guns, they fired first, we went in after them and took them out.' But that is not the way it was. There was a thing in

Alana Burke (contemporary photo overleaf) was an 18-year-old accounts clerk on Bloody Sunday, the eldest of a family of 10 from the Bishop Street area. She was crushed by an armoured personnel carrier in the car-park of the Rossville Street flats. Now separated and the mother of two boys, Alana Burke lives in the village of Killea, just outside Derry.

Alana Burke

The Bloody Sunday Inquiry

Iraq when the Americans went in and shot 13 people. They tried to say they were gunmen. You can see the parallels.

It will never go away. Sometimes sitting in the Guildhall, the evidence was so strong and so sad and so cruel and so damning that I couldn't go back for a couple of days. But there were families there that never left, morning, noon and night. I couldn't do that. You couldn't even though you wanted to. I'm glad I wasn't in London when the soldier admitted to killing Barney McGuigan because Barney's body was thrown into the ambulance on top of me. I don't know how I would have handled that.

JIMMY DUDDY

Some members of the families went religiously every day. Only a few could manage that. Gerry Duddy, for example. He had an arrangement with his wife, fair play. There was an understanding with spouses in the rest of the families that whoever was attending had to be there for those days. Otherwise, you'd have had broken marriages galore. Each person did what they felt they could do, and that was respected.

It was only over the last year or so of the Inquiry that I began to think about Saville and the other judges and the burden that has been placed on their shoulders. If they make a farce of this, it's sending out a message to other troops around the world that it's no odds if they kill people. It's happened in Israel where they murdered all around them, and it's happened in Iraq. Saville and the two judges can send out a warning – 'You're going to pay for that.' Which is not the way it's been.

It came out during the Inquiry there was an agreement with the army that the police would never investigate killings by the army. Bloody Sunday was never investigated by the police, or the deaths of Mrs Thompson or Seamus Cusack and everybody else since. That came out of the delving, that the heads of the army were able to say to the police, 'Look, if we are going to be here and we kill people, we'll investigate it ourselves.'

You can see the result. I saw on TV the day American troops took over a school. The villagers didn't want them, so they had a protest. The Americans killed 13 or 14, some of them children of five or six. They said there was a gun battle, but what they were showing you was a school. All these people were supposed to have been firing, but there wasn't one bullet mark on the school. My mind went automatic – 'They're fucking lying, they murdered those people.' This was Fallujah. So the burden on Saville is not just to finish the deeds of Bloody Sunday, but to send a message out to every other army in the world that if you put your troops in a peace situation, you're liable to the law if they kill.

I won't feel sympathy for the soldiers if they are made to pay. I have watched too many documentaries about the training of soldiers. Soldiers are trained and indoctrinated to kill. They have a lethal weapon placed in their hand. You put them in the situation and tell them there's an amount of free rein and they will do damage. They had killed unarmed civilians over the year before Bloody Sunday – seven in one day in Belfast, one of them a priest giving the last rites to a victim. So when the paras were told from the top of the army and both the Northern Ireland and British governments to go to Derry and go in hard – what did anybody expect to happen? They all knew civilians were going to be murdered. So they are as guilty as the paras who pulled the triggers.

So hopefully something will come out of this, not just for us but for all the other families everywhere in the world that these things have happened to. The military everywhere must be made to know that they are going to be accountable.

JEAN HEGARTY

I know it's been said but I don't think the Inquiry resembled a truth and reconciliation commission. I'm not sure what I would expect from a body of that sort, anyway. At the very least, I suppose I would expect the truth, and a lot of people at Saville didn't tell the truth. I don't think reconciliation is possible either, because I don't think feelings in Derry towards the army about Bloody Sunday have changed. And the Inquiry has probably alienated the Unionist community even more.

If you are going to have inquiries, all the information needs to come out. Possibly, people's identities need protection, but aside from that, why should anything remain hidden? All of the documents should be published. The Finucane case is another where there's going to be stuff withheld.

I was listening to General Sir Mike Jackson on the TV about Iraq. He gave evidence to the Inquiry two different times, one of the few witnesses who was recalled. Now, Iraq is a whole different story, but I'm thinking to myself, He's standing there just lying the same. I think in 30 years the Ministry of Defence has learned no lessons from Northern Ireland. Even after he had to come in for questioning a second time – nothing.

If the experience had caused him to second guess himself, to think about what they've been doing elsewhere in the world, and Iraq's prob-ably not the only place, then it would've been worth it. But, even if Tony Blair gets up after Saville is published and says, 'We're sorry, blah, blah, blah ...', well, that might heal a few wounds here in Derry. Or not. But what good would it be if they turn around the next day and do the same somewhere else? What they're doing in Iraq now happened here 30 years ago.

I'm a black or white kind of person. I would at one time have been open to complete violence against terrorists, but I wouldn't be any longer because, directly or indirectly, the events of Bloody Sunday, and the violence of the response, changed a lot of stuff for Northern Ireland. I'm not convinced that the violence was absolutely necessary. I didn't grow up in Creggan. I grew up in a very mixed neighbourhood. I had this romantic notion at the back of my head that things would have evolved anyway. It might have taken twice as long, but it was evolving. That's me saying that now, when I didn't live here through the height of the violence. But I do know, we all know, a lot of people died in 30 years.

While I have no sympathy for terrorists, the establishment approach is not the right approach. It wasn't the Inquiry that changed my opinions on that. It was the incident when Canadian soldiers were involved in the horrific scandal in Somalia. That had a drastic effect on my thinking. I just could not believe that an institution could be so bad.

You see the hypocrisy when you look around. The whole Middle East issue. The US is over there doing these things because Saddam Hussein didn't live up to some sanctions that the UN imposed, while Israel just totally ignores tons of them. It really concerns me. I like the US. I like going shopping there. I love visiting there. But they're an insular people. American culture is very difficult to understand. It's all right as long as everything is going grand. When things get tough they circle the wagons, and if push comes to shove they'll be as nasty to Britain as they are to anybody else. They're a very selfish people, collectively speaking.

The English government should take a real hard look at how they handled 30 years of violence here. This city is more divided now than it was 30 years ago. I don't think there's any more understanding. I would say it's worse. One of the things I found stressing since I came back is that in everyday life I'm not meeting people from another community. I think about that. It distresses me.

For me, the experience of the Inquiry changed the experience of Bloody Sunday, because although I had been back about nine years by the time the Inquiry opened, I didn't delve into the circumstances of my brother's death until the hearings actually started. Everyday at the Inquiry I learned something new about Bloody Sunday. Very shortly after the day, I remember going to a function in Canada to do with commemorating the deaths, but I came away from it and vowed I would never go to anything like that again. I felt it was a fundraising effort for something or other and I didn't want to know. Apart from phoning twice a year, I think I was home a couple of times around the anniversary and I went to the morning service but not the march. Bloody Sunday wasn't a part of my life. So, the Inquiry was a real learning experience for me in all sorts of ways.

MICHAEL McKINNEY

We got a good lot of the truth, but there's more. There's still a lot hidden. That's the main reason I don't see this Inquiry pointing a way to deal with other atrocities.

My own approach has been straightforward. My brother was murdered and somebody has to be brought to account for that. And I mean from the top down, not just the squaddies. Somebody responsible has to be held responsible. I'm still doing everything I can to make sure that happens.

I remember years ago talking to somebody at the little office we had then in West End Park and saying, 'This is going to be big.' When we stop now and look at what was achieved, it already amounts to a success. We were told lots of times, 'You're mad.' But we did it. I was part of that. I am aware that when people see me now around the town, they associate me with Bloody Sunday and the Inquiry. I've overheard it, 'There's Mickey McKinney, Bloody Sunday.'

But I don't think I had to go through the Inquiry to have the opinions that I do. Governments use the media very tactically and they talk about terrorists and paramilitaries, but the question has to be asked, why do terrorists and paramilitaries and one thing or another exist? Governments are the people the public put in power but they don't divulge the truth to the public. Iraq, Palestine, wherever else. We all know what America's done and then they try and make themselves look squeaky clean. We all know of England's involvement in Ireland over the centuries, and then they try to make themselves look great in the eyes of other peoples. But we know what they're capable of. How many Bloody Sundays have there been in Iraq? How many other isolated cases here in Ireland where the establishment has walked free without accountability?

There's been two fights within the Inquiry. One is regarding events of Bloody Sunday; the second is taking on the establishment and insisting that it can't be above the law. That's as important as the Inquiry itself. I said at meetings and in interviews that there has been inquiries in England, Zeebrugge, Hatfield, the Heathrow runway, anything in civvy street. But when it comes to the police or the army, it's closedown. Look at Stephen Lawrence's family. Look at Deepcut – the families of those soldiers were not allowed information on how their sons or their husbands or brothers came to die. It's exactly the same tactics as here in Ireland. The minute it comes to the forces, it's a closed book.

When the Inquiry is done and dusted, I will sit down and talk to my solicitor to find out if I can prosecute, and if we can we will. Some families won't proceed down that line, but I will. My brother was murdered and I want the people responsible put behind bars. If I murdered someone 30 years ago and they got evidence on me today, they'd put me behind bars. There's no difference. I'll be giving it as much again as I have the past years.

LIAM WRAY

Our brother was fully human and as a human being was entitled to his right to life. Therefore the person that took his life should be subject to the rule of law and charged with murder. That would not only be just and fair but would also demonstrate Jim's first-class citizenship. However supposing that the soldier was brought to court, and admitted guilt and the judge reprimanded him saying, 'OK, go home now and be a good boy', our family would not be without compassion or understanding for the judge's decision.

We have lived in a situation of turmoil and conflict for 35 years. We realise that today it would be of no benefit for the person who killed our brother to serve time. That's not going to improve our lives and it certainly won't bring our brother back. But the fact that the Crown recognises that murder was committed remains important.

Other families may have different views and believe that prosecution is simply not enough, that the soldiers should be imprisoned for the murders they committed. However we feel that had that happened 30 years ago, it would have benefited society, because it might have prevented other killings by soldiers. The question remains; 'What would it achieve now, if anything?' That's reconciliation in the sense that we are reconciled to that.

And even if the establishment of the Inquiry came about as part of the manoeuvring and quid pro quo of the peace process, and was not simply the results of our own efforts, the fact remains that the British government was willing to take this step towards some sort of resolution and we in the spirit of reconciliation have to accept that.

I never thought there'd been an official, specific order. I think the soldiers that day got the nod and the wink to go in and do a job. The local brigade commander MacLennan was overruled, but he was not going to rock the boat afterwards. Then the RUC had no interest in investigating because they were part of the establishment, too, and knew that the overall intention was to support the Faulkner Unionists at Stormont. Heath and Maudling and the chief of staff all had foreknowledge, maybe not to the degree of knowing how many were going to die, but knowing there was going to be death on the streets of Derry that day. This is my belief and nothing came out in the Inquiry that led me to change it.

I don't expect that the truth about Bloody Sunday is going to come out in my time. I think we are going to get parts of the truth. The whole truth would be too difficult for the British government to swallow. I'm too long in the tooth not to realise these tribunals are not immune from political pressure. Even if the pressure is not obvious, it can be insidious, and dictate how much of the truth can be risked.

We will get a partial truth which will satisfy many and I suppose in some terms will realise 80 per cent of my dream. It will not show Widgery as a whitewash. It will show him to have been misled and that in itself will nullify the Widgery conclusions which branded my brother a gunman. I wouldn't put my shirt on it, but I think the British government will be forced into a situation where they will have to accept that my brother was not a gunman and was not in proximity to any gunmen when he was shot.

We weren't and aren't unique. I remember young Annette McGavigan, only 14, shot dead by a British soldier in our area just a few months before Bloody Sunday. I remember young Damian Harkin in the street the day he got his head crushed by a British Army vehicle and my heart bled for the people of Derry. There are countless Bloody Sundays in ones, twos and threes, and those families experienced the same pain. In fact, in recent times, probably worse. When the tribunal was looking into Bloody Sunday; these people had to go in and close the door behind them. I thought if we could just get that door open a little bit, it would give hope. They might get an answer. I know that if somebody acknowledged, 'OK, young Annette wasn't caught in crossfire, she was shot dead by a British soldier who had no right to do it, and we can't do anything about that Mrs McGavigan, but it was a tragedy', if even that was acknowledged it would be really important.

I see myself a lot older, worn out, angry and with a sense of futility – that's the worst. There was more times than enough I wanted to say, 'I am out of here, fuck this for toy soldiers.' So, each little victory along the way was an uplift, every frustration a downer.

I realised in the end that justice and truth and law are three separate entities. They are not interlaced, do not serve the one purpose, they are not three parts of one whole. The law is what is en vogue. The truth is many things to many people. Justice is a thing very few of us will see in this life.

The law is something I always believed was there to let society function so the ordinary citizen could live and work in peace, with certain rights and certain protections, with wise people and governments to help to make it function. Now I realise the law is a game. That is deflating because, even at the age I am, I like to think I'm still an eternal optimist. There are still vestiges of idealism in me, but this has been an eye-opener.

I remember looking at my dead brother and all I could see was the shell. That's all he was when he got home. It was quite a thing to take in, that such a vibrant human being wasn't there any more. If I had got a gun that day, I would have been out shooting at something.

The anger and the hatred mixed in at that moment with all other emotions just wasn't controlled. But as the weeks and years pass, you look and think: I wouldn't want to do that to anybody else. And then, maybe as part of the process that has been going on, you wonder whether there was ever a time when violence was justified. Obviously, if somebody broke in my door to hurt me, my wife and my children, I would react. But in the political situation, when there are other options available, should you resort to violence? The answer is no. It is the last resort. I think the lessons of the last 30 years, and part of the Bloody Sunday Inquiry also, is that violence is not an answer to anything. It complicates and magnifies problems.

Many people lost their lives in 1972 after Bloody Sunday. I have a fear that I contributed to that because maybe in the weeks and months after, if something happened, I might have said in anger, 'Good enough for them, they deserve all they get.' When people are standing around listening, you are encouraging them in a way that you wouldn't be aware of. I think we are all guilty of that to a degree. Which is why this peace process, whether I agree with it or not, is the right thing. Once you go down the line of taking human life, it sometimes becomes very easy to justify it, or to play the role of an idealist and say that it is for Ireland. That's a lot of nonsense. It only compounds the hatred.

I miss the Inquiry. That's sounds stupid, doesn't it? But I could hide away in it from ordinary-day things. At the start, maybe it was a chore but I was dedicated. Then it became frustrating because it was taking up so much time. When my legal team got up to specification and ahead of me, I started to feel less needed, less useful. I hated having to go every day but I was afraid to miss something. When we had recesses, we were all at sea because we were used to waiting for the next thing to come out. It was a constant roller coaster of excitement and disappointment, and easy to get addicted to. You don't realise it but you can become addicted. That's the way we were living for the years of the Inquiry.

Now the ordinary things in life have come back in the door, and dealing with them has become a bit of a drag. During the Inquiry, I never did as much reading in my life. I read constantly for six years. Now, I don't even read a book. I haven't had a newspaper in two years. I got that tired of it near the end. I just got so tired.

It annoys me now when somebody asks me about the Inquiry and the report and how it's all going. It is like the Iraq war. Why did we get into the war? You see people now thinking, I don't want to talk about the war, which is natural. People are tired, they are tired. If we get a reasonable ending, at least we can all go home and say; 'Well there you are. We had to prove our relatives innocent. It took 33 years, a long walk, but not alone.'

GERALDINE DOHERTY

I have been into it so long that it just comes naturally to me now. I have ones saying to me, 'Oh, we saw you in the papers again', but I never take it on. There isn't a day I don't get up and start thinking about the Inquiry. I think a lot about your man, Paddy Ward, who came out with all that palaver about my uncle and a tray of nail bombs and how he gave him nail bombs and my uncle never gave them back, and about how he was this superman, popping up here and everywhere and shooting down a helicopter. It was a total disgrace. It made me really angry that one of our own would go in and tell lies like that to blacken people. It makes me all the more set on making sure the truth comes out. You can't let lies like that pass.

I get on with my own, normal life, but I suppose the Inquiry has changed me a bit. I felt that difference when I was the families' speaker at the 25th anniversary march. There was about 15,000 people there, and I remember thinking as I stepped up, 'Jesus, I'm never going to get through this', and I said to myself, 'You are doing this for your uncle.' Then I spoke to him and I said, 'Look, Uncle Gerald, just be beside me and get me through this, help me make sure I don't let you down.' Gerry Kelly was on the platform, and Mark Durkan, and Eamonn McCann introduced me. When I went forward to the microphone, I felt him beside me, and the nervousness left me, and the calm came across me and I got through it. I was really emotional, but I just took my time and I got through it. I felt a bit different about myself afterwards.

I do have a sense of Gerald now, of a jolly, happy-go-lucky fellow full of fun and having a laugh. I think about the fact that he should be here, should have been married and had children, my nieces and nephews. I see him in long hair, although he was just out of prison when he was murdered and had short hair. I see him the way he was in the photographs, a tall, skinny fellow with a mop of long hair. I imagine him happy-go-lucky because that's the way my mum describes him, and from the stories she tells: of him pouring her good perfume down the toilet because he thought it was air freshener. I keep him in my mind like that, my mum shouting, 'God, I'll kill you', and him laughing his head off. I'm happy I have done as much as I have been able to make sure the lies they told about him didn't last, to make sure he is remembered as he truthfully was.

MAURA YOUNG

People felt a great sense of relief at the end of the Inquiry. They stood their ground. They were able to tell what they knew. At the end of the day, that helps you. When it happened, there was no counselling. People kept it in. Nobody in our house talked about it because they were protecting me. The two older boys did all the business for Widgery. When Leo took the stand at Widgery, they more or less called him a liar. It killed my parents that Widgery said John had a gun. The whole world was told that my brother was out to take somebody's life.

When I first became involved in the campaign, I discovered other people felt the same. You were able to sit and talk about how you were feeling. For 20-odd years we had all been beating ourselves up. I'd never known Leo's full story. I got snips here and there but never heard how he felt, or about how he went in the car to take Gerald Donaghey to the hospital and was stopped and arrested. He didn't even know until he was let out the next day that Gerald Donaghey had died and that John was dead, too. They never told him his brother was dead. There was some big psychologist came from America doing some kind of paper on post-traumatic stress. That was the first time Leo did an interview and it was shocking to hear him speak about his emotions. When the Inquiry started he went every day and he got more and more involved, and it helped him. We can see a difference.

The only thing I am sorry about is my parents weren't here to see it. That's what kept me going – for them. I cried hard the first day the Inquiry opened in the Guildhall. My mother went to an awful lot of meetings. She was very strong. The fact it was now actually happening and she wasn't there roused feeling in me. I knew then, yes, however this works out, I will fight.

The evidence clarified a lot. The paras did go in and murder people. You have to show the world. You just can't let people run amuck. They did it in Cyprus. They are still doing it now, getting away with violence and then others taking to violence because they have got away with it. I don't see any point in using violence. I never did. If you have the gift of the gab you can get there quicker than throwing a stone. But, of course, not everybody has that.

It could take over your life, the Guildhall. Morning noon and night, going in, listening to people, then analysing what people said, arguing over what lawyers said. For years, that was everything.

CAROLINE O'DONNELL

Coming up to the time when he knew he was going to have to give evidence, my mammy kept saying, 'It didn't kill your father the first time, but it is going to kill him now.' But he went and did it and got over it. My father's opinion is that Widgery was a whitewash whereas this one is going to be a massive apology but with a big 'but'.

My father was actually shot but then sustained head injuries because afterwards they gave him a terrible handling. His head injuries were more threatening than his bullet wound. When he came home he was really changed from the whole trauma.

He was in total dread of having to go into the Guildhall in front of people and be cross-examined. His blood pressure got really high. My daddy wouldn't have dwelt on Bloody Sunday. It was never his life the way it was for some people. My father completely divorced himself from it, never got involved in it, just buried it. That was his way of dealing with it.

So we were never brought up in turn to dwell on what had happened. If my father had been murdered, I suppose my views would be different. My opinion as regards what should happen now – whether forgiveness and reconciliation are possible – are probably different from others because of my different circumstances.

I know my father and I know he wouldn't have been out with a gun. My father was shot to be murdered. But because of the way we were reared, we weren't bitter. You were so innocent when you were 13 back in the 70s, when there was no such thing as trauma.

If my father had been murdered, my mother would have been left with six children, which is what happened to a lot of families.

KATE AND PATRICK NASH

Patrick: It does make you look at other situations differently because you start to see that what really happened is not always what the TV is throwing out at you. It is all moves within moves.

I personally would like to see prosecutions for murder, and not just of the ordinary foot soldier. I feel prosecutions should go higher up. Edward Heath knew what was happening and I feel he should be prosecuted. After all, they still chase Nazi war criminals. Whether they should do time would be a matter for the courts. It's not out of malice, but just a conviction that if you commit a crime you have to pay and there's a lot of people should be paying.

I think, too, there should have been a hell of a lot more heard at the Inquiry. There should have been a lot more about Altnagelvin, about what happened there on the day, bodies taken in and then taken out again, bodies photographed in the morgue by British soldiers. There's probably stuff we will never know. I left feeling there was other stuff we should have been saying. It just wasn't completed for me.

I am frightened to ask how some of the other families have come through. There's a couple are not too well. The rest, I wouldn't dare ask. I don't know if I can explain what it has done to me or my sisters. I don't know the finish of it. Somebody comes on and gives evidence and its all buzz. Then the next one comes on and, Jesus, you hit the deck.

Kate: The highs and the lows were more so in London because that's where the soldiers gave their evidence. It was harder for us in London. Maybe easier for them but harder for us. I don't believe we were the important ones to the people behind the Inquiry anyway. This was something they were doing for their own reasons. You could speculate. A lot of people would put us down as paranoid. It's not paranoia. We know the tricks and games governments play. We learnt a lot about MI5 and how that crowd works. No wonder you'd be paranoid. It would be very hard to trust anything because you know the people running the country are saying one thing and doing another. It makes you look over your shoulder. I think all the Inquiry did for me was completely take away my trust. I would be looking at things with suspicion. I view everybody outside my family with suspicion, wondering what motive they have, which is a terrible way to be. The world isn't as nice a place as you used to think. Getting my brother killed, that was hard to deal with. But now through this Inquiry, you've found out things like them looking to drop a bomb in Creggan and wanting to turn off the water to the Bogside. When you realise they were sitting actually thinking about things like that, you look on all things with suspicion.

The Inquiry didn't help at all in easing pain or hurt, either. I don't know what it did except cost a lot of money. It killed my trust. I don't think I have had an ordinary life anyway. It should have been an ordinary life but what happened back then consequently directed the way my life was going to be. My mother was ill. I looked after her for seven years. My father wasn't fit to look after her after Bloody Sunday. She blamed my father. She blamed him because he survived. She wanted my brother back, not her husband, and my father accepted that blame. He carried the blame until he died five years ago. He never blamed the soldiers, he blamed himself. He thought he could have stopped it somehow. Then, in turn, I looked after my father for seven years until he died. He suffered very badly with post-traumatic stress, and you pick up on that. It was bound to affect me living in such close proximity to him. There were days if there was a helicopter in the sky, he thought he saw paratroopers dropping out of them. He might only have been like that for a few hours, but it could have been a few days. He had the fear in his bedroom and I had no life because of it. What happened that day directed the way I was going to live my life and it wasn't ordinary.

For many years, I have yearned for a quiet mind. Just maybe your general worries, your children or your grandchildren. But I worry about all sorts of other things that really shouldn't be interfering in my life. Government agencies and hospitals. I am not always in the best of health and if I have to go to a hospital it is suspicion, always suspicion, because I feel a whole lot of people like that let us down at the time. I am not talking about ordinary Derry people. I mean people in the hospitals. All sorts of rules and regulations broke down. Of course, that's brushed over as well.

There was a lot of things I would have wanted to come out at the Inquiry that were never spoken about. How come the soldiers were able to leave bodies in Altnagelvin and then come back and take them out again? If you hand dead bodies in, they belong to the coroner by law. That didn't happen on that occasion. The soldiers were able to drag those bodies back out again, and God knows what. There is a lot of questions that remain unanswered. There is a whole lot of people out there that have been able to hide in the dark. They have been able to stay behind a cloak.

TERESA McGOWAN

When Mr Clarke at the start read out the reports of the soldiers' statements, he said it was very unusual that Mr McGowan claimed he was shot down there at Block 2 of the Rossville Flats, but when he was taken to the hospital later, he was taken from his own house, which was something like five miles away. It was the way Mr Clarke said this which was so worrying, because another soldier gave evidence about seeing three gunmen up around Celtic Park. Two of them were shot and the other boy got them away in a car. My house is very near Celtic Park, so it worried me sick that they would say he must have been the gunman. I thought that's what they were thinking. I knew the reason he was brought to the house was because people who were driving the injured to hospital were getting stopped and arrested by the soldiers. But in the book Don Mullan wrote, there were photos of young Gilmour lying with a crowd around him, and my son looked and said, 'There is my daddy beside Hugh Gilmour.' And it was, plain as day. Danny had a good bush of hair and you could pick him out. I got the photo enlarged and when I went to give my statement to the Inquiry solicitors, I had it in my handbag. I brought the photo out and one of the men said, 'That's him there.' He was able to pick him out and that was 30 years before. He still had the good hair. I thought, 'Thank God he was in that photo.'

All these little things helped. Danny's solicitor stood up when they were trying to identify people in the photo and said, 'That is Mr McGowan there beside Gilmour in the photograph.' That was the proof he was there. And then, as evidence went on, one man said he saw his workmate, Danny McGowan, being carried away. Then another girl came forward and said she saw him. I just thought to myself, 'God is great, people can remember.'

Most people didn't realise all the things that went on. That girl, Peggy Deery, I remember her growing up, she had a massive family and their father died just before Bloody Sunday. How did those wains carry on? My family was lucky. They still had Danny and I was still there. I was pregnant on Bloody Sunday and I remember looking out the window at the march. Little did they know what was in front of them. The annual march still comes down the road, but Danny never went to a march after it.

I know a fella who went up who was married to a niece of mine. Years before Bloody Sunday, his car was outside his mother-in-law's when there were two fellas shot. There was an army checkpoint at the bottom of the street, the army was shot up and the car got riddled. One of the barristers from the army asked him, did he know this fella that was shot dead years back when his car got riddled? It had nothing to do with Bloody Sunday. He said, 'No.' Anna, my niece, said, 'Do you see the way they brought that from away back to see if he was involved in anything?' You never know what to say. It could implicate you in things.

I remember Danny telling me about being shot. Danny didn't actually go on the march, but he saw the march coming. I think he had been in the Derry City Club in Bishop Street. He said there was that big of a crowd on the Lecky Road, he went on down the Wells instead and came out the lane. My young brother was there and Danny chased him. Then Danny went on down to the Flats and then he heard the bullets. The people were all rush-ing through the gaps to get out and he had to stand between Block One and Two. He remembered wee Gilmour getting brought around the corner and the wee boy just collapsed. They were all kneeling round him. Every-body was saying a prayer but the wee boy was already dead. He said the only thing he regretted was that they cleared to go and get shelter. He really felt bad that they cleared and scattered and left.

Then there was more shooting. Danny ran under the canopy of the shops. There was another man calling for help and he went over to the back of Joseph's Place. Danny said he heard calling, 'Over here, over here Danny', but when he got over it was packed. There was no room for him. He went to turn to try to get to the steps and he got shot in the leg, so he was brought home. I remember Danny lying on the settee and then the ambulance came.

It does change how you look at other places. Look at Iraq. I am sorry for those people, even the ones that are shooting little children. I pray for them every day and I hope to god it ends. The way we are here in North-ern Ireland people take one side or the other, so who are we to judge people over there? Maybe Saddam was a bad brute and is well out of the road, but who are the ones coming on, what kind of people are they? You think of the people murdered on Bloody Sunday, and then you think that every day in life there are people on buses and people walking by getting blown up and all that. How can they do that, and take their own life with it? I was looking at a film about America. I couldn't look at it. It was about President Bush and I was thinking, 'Is this made up or is it really true?' I can't get over the fact that this can go on. I suppose it's all about money, but here and there and everywhere, I just wish it was all over.

The thing is, if Danny had been living on, I would have been more into it. But now that it's finished, it's an area in my life that will be closed too. I want it done. We have plenty of books and papers in the house if the wains and the grand-wains want to know. It's all there for them to see. But for me it is finished.

MICKEY BRIDGE

Anyone who sat down and went back through the evidence couldn't come to any conclusion but that Bloody Sunday was instigated by the British government as a matter of policy and implemented as such. The people involved in the killing were given honours by the Queen. Now the very least that can be said about Bloody Sunday is it was controversial, and yet they chose to decorate those people. Bloody Sunday was state-instigated. The rest is waffle.

That affects my views, obviously. Looking around, knowing what I know about the way the world works, it seems to me now that violence to change things politically is justified. There's never been change that hasn't been forced by violence, not that I know of. Violence to overthrow something corrupt is justified, in a contained way. The way it's happening in Iraq is horrendous.

I wasn't living in great hurt over the years. I had come to accept Widgery's report. To be more accurate, I didn't accept it, I just found myself in a situation where I could do fuck all about it. But when this Inquiry came about, I thought it was the proper time and I tried to get it as right as I could. In that, I didn't succeed. The Inquiry has been very far from satisfactory.

The end of the Inquiry put a dampener on things. Before the Inquiry, I would have been working seven days a week. But the amount of work I've done in the years of the hearings is almost non-existent. It eats you up, or rather I allowed it to eat me up. A few of the others were the same.

One of the things that struck me during the Inquiry was that people took it for granted that the wounded must have had a good knowledge from the start of what had happened because we were involved. But we didn't know what had happened. In the hospital, we were prisoners. There were four of us in the room, Joe Friel, shot in the chest in Glenfada Park, Alex Nash, who was hit in the arm and the stomach at the barricade, Patrick Campbell and myself. We were in there and there were soldiers in plain clothes posted with guns at the door. How could we know what the position was? There was hardly a word said between us the first day. Joe Friel and myself had operations that night, so we were out for that time. The rest of the time, we lay there within ourselves. We were in the dark until the newspapers came the next day.

When I was brought into casualty they put me into a room, then Joe Friel came in. There were people being wheeled past the room right, left and centre, but I was concentrating on Joe Friel because he was in the room with me and I thought he was going to die. As far as I was concerned, there had been two or three people shot.

A couple of days later, one of the nurses went down and brought a TV up so we could see the funerals. They wouldn't give us an aerial, so I got it working with a dismantled coat hanger. It wasn't until then we got the full picture. There was nearly murder in the hospital then. I was trying to get out of bed. Bubbles was on crutches and wanted to get at the soldiers guarding us. They were taken away very promptly.

All the time he was in the hospital, Alex Nash never opened his mouth. It was there that he learned that his son was dead. I'll tell you something else, Alex Nash was shot twice. He was shot in the arm, and he was shot across the stomach. They told him he had been hit in the stomach by a rubber bullet. But I saw the wound. It was a lead bullet which skimmed him. I know it's not part of the official history of Bloody Sunday, but I don't give a monkey's. He was shot twice.

I never talked about any of it to my sisters or my brother. For years, I had it in my head that if I hadn't run out there wouldn't have been any more killing. There's no logic to that, but I had it in my head. I honestly don't know how it changed me or didn't in the long term. There were too many things happening. It affected my family life, that's for certain. I married a woman from Eglinton, and there was a time her father wouldn't look at me. I had to give up a job delivering coal in the Waterside. I couldn't show my face. Once people knew I was from Bloody Sunday, they believed I must have been a gunman. I remember being in Belfast and coming into the train station and being paranoid somebody would recognise me from Bloody Sunday.

After Motorman – the huge British operation the summer after Bloody Sunday, when they re-entered the Bog and Creggan – after that I was arrested more times than enough. I was once arrested six times in a week. Mostly it was soldiers, not the police, although I was arrested a few times by them as well. I moved out from Creggan to Coshquin, and Bloody Sunday would be thrown up at me regularly at the checkpoint there. After the bomb at the checkpoint, although I wasn't living in Coshquin at that point, I was arrested and held for two days. They just put the two together, wounded on Bloody Sunday, lived in Coshquin. I taxied for a while in the 1990s, and I would get it when I was checked through at roadblocks or whatever. That didn't affect me a lot. It just got my back up. But it let me know Bloody Sunday was following me.

KAY DUDDY

It was a strange kind of a feeling. It half took over your whole life. It was as if your family life and your home came second to the Inquiry. If you were at home you wanted to be at the Inquiry, and if you were at the Inquiry, you were thinking about the things you should have been doing at home. It nearly drove me nuts. You wanted to be there 24/7. It was so important to me and to my family. It became part of what I meant to people. I was coming back from the hospital one day and this lady said, 'You're not the other girl, you're the Bloody Sunday woman.'

You look around the world now and you see things all the time which make you think of Bloody Sunday. I think it is a sad fact that it is the innocent who always suffer. I never understand why they call them civil wars because there is nothing civil about them.

It does seem that wherever there are monstrosities happening, the British government is part of it. I thought they got off the hook the time they showed the photographs about maltreating prisoners in Iraq. The Yanks got the brunt of it but I am sure the Brits were at it as much, because they did it here, big time.

At the end of the day, it's about my brother being murdered. I look at that picture. I see Jackie's face and those wee boxing gloves and that wee smile. We put his 50th birthday in the paper in July and I thought, 'That's all we can do for you now, a wee memorial in the paper, people will say a prayer for you on your 50th birthday, when we should have been out partying with you.' It is hard no matter what you have been through or what you have tried to do about it. It is the everyday things, the wee family things that get you.

JOHN KELLY

I didn't focus until the Inquiry on the fact that there were other Bloody Sundays as well, and that violence everywhere is a means of destroying the innocence of people. There are other ways forward in relation to how problems can be overcome, other than the gun or the bomb. You don't achieve anything from violence except pain and torment for the ones left behind. If I look at the families attending the Inquiry I can see the pain they are still enduring after all these years. The Derry community too, still carries the trauma. When I go into a pub for a pint I don't want to talk about Bloody Sunday, but people come up and say, 'How's it going for you?' They are still concerned.

Some people from the families couldn't deal with the pain of listening to the evidence every day or going to London and seeing the guys who pulled the triggers. Maybe I have become hardened. The emotion that went along with the Inquiry was very difficult for some people.

I think the experience has changed me. I was brought up to show total respect for barristers and lawyers and doctors and priests and stuff like that. Now I see they are no different to me and I am no less than anybody else. I can look anybody in the eye and say, 'Well, you are this or that but we are the same.'

The process re-enlightened me to the way people feel about Bloody Sunday. I feel I have got plenty out of it myself, out of the simple fact that we have had a new Inquiry and seen the guys who perpetrated the killings brought in front of us, and seen civilians, hundreds, literally, after all the years, having the opportunity for the first time to tell their story. That's so important to the families. All that coming out helped to lift the weight off their shoulders. I have seen the way it lifted a burden from the civilian witnesses themselves, too. I gave evidence myself. I had that opportunity to tell Saville what my feelings were, and to pass onto him the feelings of my mother. That was a great relief to me. She hadn't been on the march, but she'd gone looking for Michael. The reason she would have watched him more carefully than the rest of us was that when he was three he took some kind of virus and went into a coma. My mother had us all around the bed saying the rosary. She walked it backwards and forwards to the Waterside hospital twice a day for the duration – in those days there was no real traffic, plus she couldn't afford buses. Eventually he came around and recovered. So, naturally, when it came to the troubles she was more inclined to oversee Michael. On Bloody Sunday he asked was it okay for him to go on the march and she refused. But eventually, through persuasion from the likes of myself, she gave in and let him go. She followed the march to keep an eye on him.

When the paras moved into Rossville Street she was in her sister's flat in Kells Walk and looked out the back window and saw him. She shouted to him but he didn't hear her and ran on like everybody else at the time. Then the shooting began. She didn't know Michael was shot when she made her way home. Somebody gave her a lift up to Broadway. 'A terrible day, a terrible day', she was saying, terrible things happening down there, not realising that Michael had been shot. When she got to the house there were people saying Michael had been shot in the ankle.

All my brothers-in-law and a couple of sisters were at the march. Myself and two brothers-in-law accompanied Michael to the hospital where he was declared dead. We had to contact home to get my father to identify his body. As the oldest brother, I could have done that, but for some reason, I didn't. After we went through everything at the hospital, we went home. I remember saying to my mother, 'Michael is dead' and total bedlam after that.

I remember the night the bodies were released. He was laid out in the back room where he had slept. I think it was three or four o'clock in the morning when she dived into the room and bodily lifted Michael out of the coffin. She caught us unawares she moved that fast for a wee stumpy woman, crying, 'Michael son, Michael son.' We had to restrain her and place Michael back into the coffin.

Even now, I don't remember the day of the funerals, although I see photographs of my mother crying in my aunt's arms. For a long time afterwards, we couldn't let her out of the house because we didn't know what she would do or where she would go. There was one day she was found going up Broadway towards the cemetery with a blanket under her arm and someone asked her, 'Where are you going with the blanket?' and she said, 'I'm going to place it over Michael's grave to keep him warm.' There was snow on the ground. Other times she went missing and we would find her in the cemetery sitting along with Mrs Wray, chatting away about their sons. It came to the stage she was unable to look after herself and her family. The older girls took over.

My mother was a family woman. She bore children and she brought us all up in a fair and decent and controlled way, to respect our elders and do what we were told. If one got a sweet we all got a sweet. If one got a pair of socks, everyone got a pair of socks. How she did it, I don't know. My father didn't work very much at the time. He dealt with Michael's death in his own way. He didn't really show his emotions, but after his death in 1991 we found a wallpaper sample book and in it was all the photographs of Bloody Sunday. Even up to a year ago, we didn't know that he had written a letter to his sister in America a couple of days after Bloody Sunday explaining everything that happened. We never knew that. This was the way he was. After all the pain of how Bloody Sunday affected our family, I think it created an anger within me, and determination that if any possible chance came along that we could possibly do something about it, then we would. Getting the Inquiry fulfilled that to a certain extent.

Now it's come to the situation where I want to be able to walk away and surround myself with my own family or whatever else I am going to do. I hope to walk away with a smile on my face and be able to say at least I did my best for my brother. I was one of a group of people who took on the British establishment and achieved something massive, even if I'm not yet sure exactly what that is or what it's going to be.

I have been to places I never thought I'd be and spoken to people I never thought I'd speak to. It's been my job and it's been fascinating. I became so engrossed in it. I remember one time I was dying with the flu waking up and Michael's photograph was looking at me and I heard myself saying out loud, 'That's the way to do it, That's the way to do it.' I don't know what I was talking about, except that through the sickness I was still trying to work out what to do about Bloody Sunday.

It's been a private thing, too. I don't discuss Bloody Sunday in the house. I haven't been wrapped around it within my own home. It was when I came to meetings or had to travel somewhere that I would become a total part of the Bloody Sunday issue. Inside the house I would keep it inside myself. I started taking documentation home with me one time, but I stopped that. I don't need that. I would need to build another house, anyway. I keep the separation between the family and the issue. You will find that most families are the same. I have nine sisters and another brother and I would keep them informed. When my mother was alive, I would have gone up to her on a regular basis and told her what was going on.

My sister Sophia attended the Inquiry in Derry every day, and she went to London steady, which was brilliant. Sophia was there for our family as well.

For those who attended every day, there was a massive void when the Guildhall shut. People have to find a way of dealing with that. I don't know what's going to happen to me. I will be glad to move on, knowing we have done a great job. We have the Brits on the run, no two ways about it, and they know it.

KEVIN McDAID

The Inquiry and all the activity around it made it easier to talk more openly about our experiences. At one meeting in the Calgagh Centre I was able to relate what I had seen to the guy who was sitting beside me. A man was up talking about what happened. I knew the guy had been there because he was one of the wounded, but he didn't know I was there. And he looked at me and I looked at him and I said, 'That's wrong what he is saying up there.' And he says, 'How do you know?' and I says, 'I was there', and he says, 'Whereabouts?' and I told him and what I had seen. And he had seen what I had seen. That sort of thing helped to bring the process along. I'm sure it helped a lot of members of other families. You knew there were other people to say they'd seen what you had seen.

But the Inquiry didn't happen the way Tony Blair promised. He said it

Kevin McDaid (right), a painter and decorator, was one of a family of 12 from the Bogside. He was 17 on Bloody Sunday, three years younger than Michael (left), a bar manager, who was shot and killed at the Rossville Street barricade. Kevin McDaid is married with four children and lives in the Hatmore Park area of Derry.

would be wide open, and it wasn't. You had the Home Office and the MoD taking the Inquiry to court to prevent this coming out, that coming out. Look at the soldiers' statements going back to 1972, contradicting themselves and covering up, all with the help of government lawyers. It was the same during this Inquiry: 'We can't let his out, we can't let that out.' The disappearance of the photographs taken on the day. The helicopter footage that couldn't be found. The MoD destroying some of the weapons which were used, when they had already been told by the Inquiry they were needed.

So the full truth hasn't come out. The evidence has been open from our point of view because we had nothing to hide. But when it came to the army, they were not there to tell the truth. And without the truth how can you have reconciliation? It won't happen.

We always knew the truth as regards Michael. We had the photographs of him standing there after Michael Kelly had been shot. I was just on the side of the barricade. The people who were there know what happened. My brothers and sisters, my sons and daughters and their children, our family in general, we want some sort of closure. Otherwise, it will continue into the next generation. I'm not bitter, not compared to how I was, but there has to be closure.

Most of the people killed were only young guys. Most of them were working. They weren't layabouts. Michael worked from before he left school until the day he was shot. He was running John Bradley's pub and he was only 19 years of age, which was a big responsibility. Why were they killed? Were the soldiers told to do it? Or did they just know what they were expected to do? The ordinary soldier could turn round and say, 'Well, he told me' or 'He told me.' How far does it go? All the way back to Heath? Somebody has to answer.

This Inquiry hasn't been like Widgery. The British government can't be seen to be doing what they did in 1972. This time, there's more people looking on than just people with a local point of view. They have to put on a better act than they did in 1972, and that's something. It's out there now for people to see what the families went through, and the whole town, and the whole of Northern Ireland. This war could have been over donkey's years ago if Bloody Sunday hadn't happened. At least, it wouldn't have lasted so long. It's had a helluva lot of repercussions.

JOE MAHON

I agree with the Palestinians but I don't agree with the suicide bombers. If they want to kill Israelis then kill Israeli soldiers. I don't believe that anybody has a right to go into a café and blow people up because they are Jewish. I don't believe the Israelis should go into a camp and kill Palestinians either. It's the same as Bloody Sunday. We were shot because we were Irish and because we were Catholics. That's the reason. That's the same thing as putting a bomb on a bus of Israelis or Americans or Iraqis or blowing up street markets with car bombs. In a war, soldiers should fight soldiers.

If they throw the evidence back in our face now, they deserve all they get. I don't care who is listening, they deserve all they get. They have a chance to come clean and say, 'Listen, we were at fault, the boys ran amuck, jumped orders, they weren't supposed to come into the Bogside.' It happened long enough ago now. If they came forward and said that they were wrong, then, for the world's media it would be a two-day wonder. But I believe the people of Derry would be happy. On the other hand, if all the evidence that's come out is thrown away, then they deserve all they get.

EILEEN GREEN

You thought you knew everything about Bloody Sunday, but you found out you didn't. I learnt a lot about Bloody Sunday, and a lot about myself as a person, too. I am stronger, because I have dealt now with every part of Bloody Sunday.

As for our family, when the Report is published, that's it. If, for instance, they were to come out and say Paddy Doherty was murdered, then the due process of law would have to take over. That process would have nothing to do with us. Even if there is a finding of murder, and even if there is due process after that, I don't believe any para will do a day. That doesn't mean they cannot be made accountable. The findings will make them accountable. But that's it. The Report is the last kick of the ball. At that, this family is finished.

I suppose in a way we were lucky. You can look now at other things happening, here or anywhere in the world, and say, 'Yes, those people deserve an Inquiry.' But you know they are not going to get one. Not one like this one anyway. I don't think they'll ever grant another Inquiry like this.

DAMIEN DONAGHEY

At the start I wasn't really aware of how significant it was, but when you saw the amount of evidence and submissions and the files that the solicitors and barristers had put together, it was unbelievable. The biggest in Europe. It's like you're in history. You never think you're part of history but as the years go on, you see it better.

The people of Derry supported every family. They knew what the

Damien Donaghey, now 49, a window-cleaner, was the first person shot on Bloody Sunday, wounded by a sniper as he stood on waste ground on William Street. The bullet struck him on the thigh. Damien Donaghey lives with his wife and four children in the Creggan.

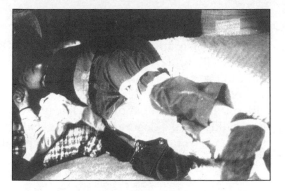

families went through because they went through it themselves. People gave evidence that they had lived with for 30 years. Fair play to them.

Some lawyers were on fees of up at £1,750 a day and some of them didn't even speak, but that wasn't our fault. Gregory Campbell was attacking our barristers but he wasn't hitting at the soldiers' barristers who were getting more. It annoyed me at the start but then I got to the stage where I just didn't care, because he was right in a way. Was I getting £1,750 a day? I was going down to the Inquiry every day, too. On both sides, barristers and solicitors made money out of it. But that's happening all the time. Mansfield, they said, was on £1,700 a day but he was getting £2,500 a day for murder trials in London. Money wouldn't mean much to people like that. It wouldn't matter what Campbell said, even if they earned millions a day, he wasn't going to stop criticising anyway because it wasn't really the money that was getting at him.

Before, I wouldn't have been able to speak a lot without stuttering. Then I seemed to get used to it. In Derry and London I was able to give interviews without a second thought. Because you knew you were innocent you didn't have to care what you said.

I never saw anybody killed because myself and Johnny Johnston were shot earlier. But what I know happened was that it was all young people they were shooting dead. Johnny Johnston was old, Peggy Deery was a woman, but the biggest majority were young men. They knew what they were doing. It is the same thing in Palestine. It is all young people they are killing. How many inquiries would you need over there?

It isn't to say the Inquiry changed my worldview. All you have to do is look at the TV. Look at Iraq now and the amount of people that are being killed everyday. The Iraq war has probably been for oil, but with Palestine it is about more, because the Israelis are more on line with America against the Palestinian people. The whole world has gone wrong.

JOHNNY CAMPBELL

I wouldn't like anything to happen to anybody that happened to my father. To me, it's futile. There's an easier way round things. You can sort it, or if you can't sort it you can walk away from it. Life is too sacred. It's not for anybody to decide to end anybody else's life. I think Saville can only come out with one thing. I don't know which way others will decide to go, but I think we should just take closure then. If we get all the names cleared, and the guilt put where the guilt should lie, we should put it all behind us and move on.

REGINA McKINNEY

I f I hadn't had the Inquiry I would have cracked up. It was a source of strength. It opened up a lot for me as regards other families and Derry itself. Growing up, I used to think, 'My daddy was my daddy, not anybody else's.' But listening to the evidence gave me an understanding of how the people reacted together.

Our family tried to have a private grief. As children, we couldn't under-

Regina McKinney (far right) was the third eldest of eight children of Gerry McKinney (right), 35, a wrought-iron worker and dance hall manager. He had blessed himself and put his hands in the air when confronted in Abbey Park by soldiers, one of whom then shot him dead. Now 42, Regina McKinney is widowed with two daughters and lives in the Galliagh area of Derry.

Regina McKinney

stand why everyone else seemed part of it. It was difficult to try and grieve for a father but not get to do it within yourself. I can understand a lot more now. It was quite difficult as children, especially regarding Barney. I would have a soft spot for him and his family. At that time, I would have been t raumatised over Barney, maybe more than over daddy.

Because of the horrificness of the way Barney died, I kind of thought that my daddy died clean. My daddy was still in one piece. He was shot with his hands up. I was proud the way my father died, not that he was shot but that he had his hands in the air, that he had nothing in his hands, that he did not retaliate. To me he was a hero. Every one of them was in their own right. Heroes. But with Barney, for him to be killed in that horrible way – I was glad that my daddy didn't die like that. So your heart then begins to go out to other people.

My mother and Barney's wife got to know each other very well. We used to go out together. It must have been terrible for the McGuigans. It was terrible for us, too, but when you look at other people you begin to see, 'Gosh, think what they have had to go through.' You begin to realise that it wasn't one singular thing. It wasn't just my daddy. It was about every single person shot on Bloody Sunday and everybody close to them. It was about everybody.

I would go to the Bloody Sunday Centre and I would see Kay and Bernie and Linda Roddy. It turns out that her mother-in-law's wee brother is buried in the same grave as my daddy. Things like that come to light when you get to know one another. What happened among and between us I don't think will ever be severed. I would feel a protective thing as regards the families, knowing what I know now. I'd stand up for them. For the families as families, as a unit. I'd back them to the hilt.

The only thing I want out of it now is for the men who were shot to go down in history as innocent. I think that is the only truth that we need. A lot of pride has to be swallowed in Northern Ireland, on all sides. There's nobody going to have everything they want out of all this. If the soldiers and the government were to stand up and take responsibility, that, too, would go down in history. They would show themselves to be better people. The Bloody Sunday soldiers are going to have to stand before God. I believe there will be a final judgement. My father will be justified.

Afterword

Seven months after Bloody Sunday, the First Battalion of the Parachute Regiment killed again in Northern Ireland. This time it was two Protestant men from the Shankill Road area of Belfast who had the misfortune to stray into their sights. Robert McKinnie, 49, and Robert Johnston, 50, were shot dead in the Shankill on 7 September 1972. There was a flurry of political interest at the time, but it soon passed.

The killings were referred to at the Bloody Sunday Inquiry in October 2002, during questioning of Soldier 027 by Seamus Treacy QC, for a number of the families. Soldier 027 was among a small number of paras who had broken ranks and admitted that members of the First Battalion had, at the least, behaved improperly on Bloody Sunday.

Reporting the exchanges in the *Belfast Telegraph* on 24 October 2002, I wrote:

Treacy's intention was to try to show that what happened in Derry had arisen from a pattern of behaviour by the Paras which had been tolerated by the military authorities in the months before the Derry deaths and which continued to be tolerated afterwards. Saville intervened to cut Treacy short on the ground that the Tribunal could not draw conclusions from the Shankill incident without investigating it anew, and that this was impractical.

However, evidence already in the public domain provides a picture of how the two men died. Medical evidence to the inquest in October 1972 told that Johnston, a single, unemployed man who lived alone at Sydney Street West, died from a high-velocity bullet which struck him on the back and ripped through his heart before exiting from his chest. A number of civilian witnesses described Johnston seemingly drunk and waving his arms around at the junction of Berlin Street and Weir Street moments before he was shot. Sarah Anderson of Silvio Street said he was shouting, 'I walked these streets in my bare feet in the Thirties.'

William Greer, manager of the Wee House bar on Berlin Street, said: 'I heard him shout, "The meek shall inherit the earth." Then I heard a single shot .... The old man staggered forward and fell.'

All civilian witnesses were adamant that rioting in the area had abated some time before the shooting and that both Johnston and McKinnie had been clearly unarmed.

Robert McKinnie, an engineering worker at Mackies, known to his friends as Ritchie, was shot as he drove slowly along Matchett Street, avoiding debris from the earlier riot. Medical evidence suggested that the bullet shot off his thumb as it gripped the steering wheel and then fragmented, lacerating the arteries of his chest and entering his lung.

McKinnie had been driving his brother, Thomas, on a tour of some of their old haunts. Thomas had returned from Canada the previous day for his first visit home in 31 years. He recalled for the inquest 'a flash of white as the windscreen shattered …. Ritchie said, "Oh, I'm hit," and fell over …. I got my arms around his chest. I could feel that my hands were wet …. I started to holler …'

Eye-witnesses, including George Cree, Joe Thompson and David Beck of Matchett Street and Evelyn McIntyre and Joyce Cummins of Jersey Street, were insistent that there had been no gunshots from the car or its vicinity. All the civilian witnesses alleged that the Paras had been abusive before and after the shooting, shouting 'Orange bastards', jeering that 'at least the IRA are men', and directing obscenities towards women.

Four soldiers, 'A', 'B', 'E' and 'J', gave statements to the Royal Military Police which were presented to the inquest. All told of their unit coming under fire and of fire being returned. In an apparent description of the killing of Johnston, 'A' described two gunmen opening fire in Berlin Street with Sterling sub-machine guns. 'I saw the muzzle flashes … and heard the rounds strike near me.' He said he fired two shots in return and saw one of the gunmen fall.

In an apparent description of the killing of McKinnie, 'J ' said that he had shouted at the driver of a slow-moving car on Matchett Street to turn his lights off, that he had heard a gunshot and seen a muzzle flash to the left of the car, that a man emerged from the car carrying a rifle which he pointed at the soldiers, that he had then shot him.

Hundreds attended a protest picket at Tennent Street RUC station the following day. Ian Paisley threatened to boycott a conference at Darlington called by Secretary of State William Whitelaw if there wasn't a public inquiry. Brian Faulkner visited Tennent Street to talk to police investigators. An unofficial inquiry at West Belfast Orange Hall five days after the killings concluded that there was a 'desperate need for an independent judicial inquiry'.

Last Monday's brief mention was the first and only time the Shankill deaths have come before a judicial inquiry. 'He was a totally harmless man,' said Sarah Anderson of Robert Johnston.

'I wish to add,' said Joseph Thompson, 'that I have known the deceased Ritchie McKinnie all my life, and a more respectable person you couldn't meet.'

Following publication of the *Telegraph* piece, I contacted elected representatives of the Shankill area – from the Democratic Unionist Party, the Ulster Unionist Party and the Progressive Unionist Party – and suggested that they use the reference at Saville as a peg on which to hang a demand for an overdue investigation and acknowledgement that the two men had been wrongfully done to death. None of the representatives responded.

Some months later, two Shankill politicians were asked for help in contacting any members of the Johnston and McKinnie families still living in the area. No such help was forthcoming. A city councillor for the area explained: 'It would look like we were coming onto the Bloody Sunday band-wagon and unionists won't do that.'

Thus does the Protestant working class lose out, even unto death, from the communal politics of Northern Ireland.

Eamonn McCann